D1061235

More
Storybook
Cross-stitch

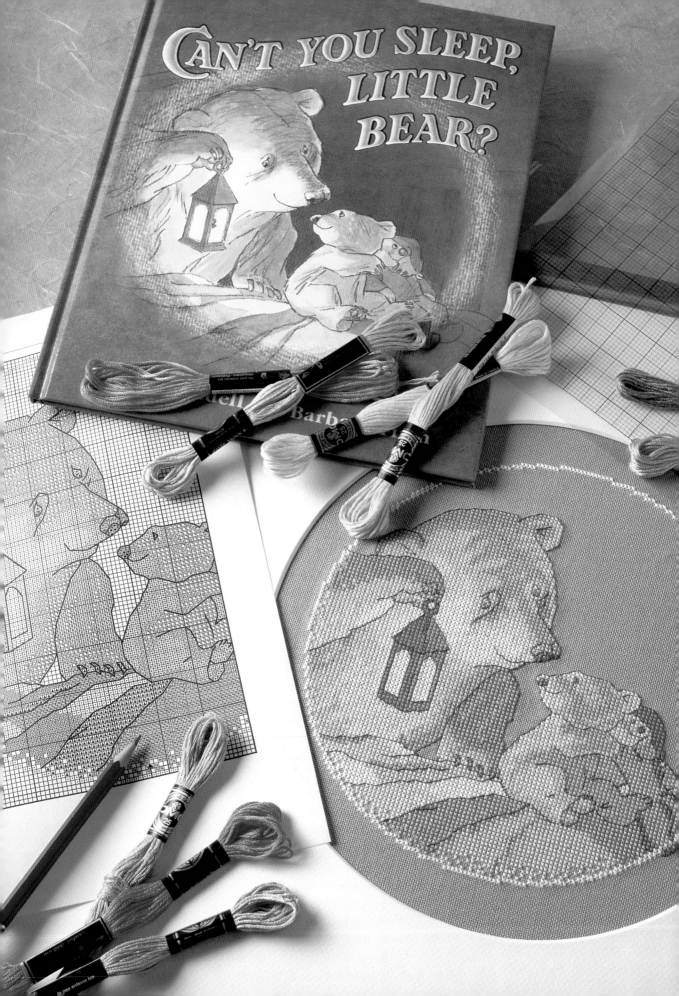

More Storybook Cross-stitch

Gillian Souter

LITTLE, BROWN AND COMPANY
Boston New York Toronto London

A LITTLE, BROWN BOOK

First published in Great Britain in 1998
by Little, Brown and Company (UK)

Created and designed by Off the Shelf Publishing,
32 Thomas Street, Lewisham, NSW 2049, Australia

Copyright © Off the Shelf Publishing, 1998
The moral right of the author has been asserted.

All rights are reserved. No part of this book nor any
pattern or part of any pattern in it may be reproduced,
manufactured or made up for resale or for any other
commercial purpose in any material form without the
express written consent of the publishers.
No part of this publication may be circulated in any form
of binding or cover other than that in which it is published and without a similar condition including this
condition being imposed on the subsequent purchaser.

A CIP catalogue record for this book
is available from the British Library

ISBN 0-316-64289-4

10 9 8 7 6 5 4 3 2 1

Produced by Phoenix Offset
Printed and bound in China

Little, Brown and Company (UK)
Brettenham House
Lancaster Place
London WC2E 7EN

Contents

Introduction

A few years ago, I wrote a book called Storybook Favourites in Cross-stitch, which included designs based on many popular children's book characters, such as Paddington, Spot, Babar and Miffy. The book was such a success, and so many of my friends pointed out all those characters I'd overlooked, that this is the result. The title—More Storybook Cross-stitch—is not, admittedly, the most original, but it does tell you what's in store. I had no trouble finding enough characters, in fact quite the opposite. Once again, there are familiar companions from decades ago—the Velveteen Rabbit, Noddy and Thomas the Tank Engine—and there are modern charmers, such as Elmer, Maisy and Postman Pat. There are also a few old friends making a guest appearance from the first book: Angelina and the creations of Beatrix Potter proved so very popular. The different styles of the original illustrators have inspired a great range of cross-stitch designs, with something to suit every taste and level of experience. As before, each design is made into a project which is sure to delight children. I hope you'll enjoy the stitching and making of these almost as much as those children will enjoy receiving them.

David McKee

ELMER AND WILBUR

Maisy goes to playschool   Lucy Cousins   *Walker*   Ande

MAISY'S HOUSE – A Pop-up and Play Book   Lucy Cousins   WALKER BOOKS

WADDELL · FIRTH   YOU AND ME, LITTLE BEAR   WADDELL · FIRTH   WALKER BOOKS

CAN'T YOU SLEEP LITTLE BEAR?

THE Complete Tales OF BEATRIX Potter   WARNE

Ned

Ned

Angelina Ballerina   Young   WARNE   ABC

NODDY GETS INTO TROUBLE   8

THE TALE OF TOM KITTEN

TOM KITTEN
PIGLING BLAND
O BAD MICE
R RABBIT
UCESTER
CZIEK

BEATRIX POTTER
THE ORIGINAL AND AUTHORISED EDITIONS
F. WARNE & Co   1   5

THE RAILWAY SERIES NO. 16
Branch Line Engines

THE RAILWAY SERIES NO. 10
Four Little Engines

THE RAILWAY SERIES NO.
Tank Engine Thomas Again

THE REV. W. AWDRY

Ange

Basic Techniques

Cross-stitch is one of the most popular of crafts and is extremely simple to learn. If you are new to this form of embroidery, this chapter will give you all the information you need to complete the projects in this book.

In cross-stitch, a pattern is transferred from a charted design to a piece of un-marked fabric. The chart is a grid of squares with symbols forming the design. A key tells you which colour of embroidery thread relates to which symbol on the chart. Working the design is simply a matter of stitching a series of crosses in the appropriate colour according to the arrangement on the chart.

Types of Fabric

Cross-stitch fabrics are evenly woven, that is, they have the same number of threads over a given distance both vertically and horizontally. Aida fabric, formed with bands of threads, is often used. There are many types of fabric woven in single threads: these can be made of various fibres but they're referred to in this book simply as linen.

The size of each stitch is determined by the number of fabric threads over which you sew and by the number of bands or threads per inch of fabric (known as the fabric count). Most fabric counts are still given in inches, even in countries which have adopted the metric system. Linen 26 has twenty-six threads per inch of fabric and

each stitch covers two threads (to prevent the embroidery thread gliding under a fabric thread) so there are thirteen stitches per inch. With Linen 30, there are fifteen stitches per inch: the larger the fabric count, the smaller the stitches will be.

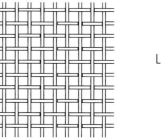

Linen

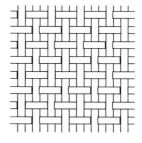

Aida

Estimating Size

The instructions for each project specify the type of fabric used to stitch it and the amount of fabric required. When you choose a fabric with a different thread count, you will need to calculate what the size of the stitched design will be. Use the following rule: finished size equals the design stitch count divided by the fabric thread count.

When using linen, you stitch over two threads. Therefore, a stitch count of 50 x 50 (i.e. 50 squares on the chart each way) must be divided by 13, if using Linen 26, or by 15 (Linen 30) and so on. Aida also comes in various counts: if using Aida 14, divide the stitch count by 14. Multiply the result by 2.5 to convert from inches into centimetres.

Preparing the Fabric

To prevent the fabric from fraying, zigzag the edges on a sewing machine or simply use masking tape which can later be removed.

Locate the centre of the fabric by folding it in half and then in half again. If you are working on a large design, mark the centre with a pin and use a coloured thread to tack from side to side and from top to bottom, each time tacking through the centre mark. This should quarter your fabric. When you start cross-stitching, make sure the centre of the design (indicated by arrows on the chart) matches the centre point of your fabric.

Embroidery Thread

Cross-stitch is generally worked in stranded cotton embroidery thread. The designs in this book have all been stitched using DMC stranded cotton. If you wish to use a different brand, match the colours shown in the pictures as closely as possible or choose your own combinations.

The key for each design lists: a symbol which appears in the chart, a corresponding DMC thread number, a colour name for easy identification, and the number of stitches to be made in that colour. It is impossible to gauge the exact amount of thread needed

but this will give an idea of the relative quantities required for each colour. As a very rough guide, a block of 100 cross-stitches on Aida 14 requires 50 cm of embroidery thread using two strands at a time.

The six strands of the embroidery thread can be split into single strands, three lengths of double strands, or other combinations. The number of strands used depends on the count of your fabric. In general, using more strands will make your finished work more vivid, but if you use too many strands they will not fit neatly within the weave of the fabric. Below is a suggested number of strands for different fabric counts. It is a good idea, though, to add an extra strand when stitching the design on a dark fabric.

Count	Cross-stitch strands	Backstitch strands
Aida 11	3	2
Aida 14	2	1
Aida 18	2	1
Aida 22	1	1
Linen 16	3	2
Linen 20	2	1
Linen 28	2	1
Linen 32	1	1

Equipment

Use a blunt needle such as a small tapestry needle that will not split the fabric threads. Match the size of the needle to the size of the hole: a size 24 needle is suitable for Linen 20 or Aida 11 whereas a size 26 needle would be appropriate for Aida 14.

You will need two pairs of scissors: a small pair for trimming threads and a pair of shears for cutting the fabric.

If you are stitching one of the larger designs, or any that require several similar shades of embroidery thread, your spare strands can easily become jumbled. To make a simple thread holder like the one pictured, cut a length of sturdy card and use a hole punch to cut holes at regular intervals. Mark the colour number and the appropriate symbol alongside the hole and tie your threads as shown.

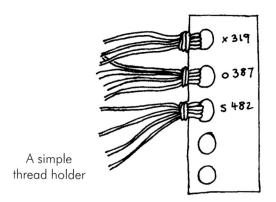

A simple thread holder

A frame or embroidery hoop will help you to stitch evenly and prevent warping, but it is not necessary for very small designs. Choose a hoop which will fit the whole design, otherwise it will damage existing stitches.

Reading the Charts

Each square on the chart represents a full cross-stitch and each symbol represents a colour as specified in the key. A heavy line indicates where to backstitch and the key will tell you which colour to use for each section of backstitching. Arrows indicate the centre of the design.

Check the instructions regarding the position of the stitching on the fabric; if there are no specific instructions, orient the fabric to match the chart and stitch the design in the centre. Find the colour represented by the centre symbol and start on that block of colour.

Cut a 50 cm length of embroidery thread and gently split it into the appropriate number of strands. Let the strands dangle and untwist.

Cross-stitching

Thread the needle with the appropriate number of strands and bring it through the fabric, leaving 2 cm of waste thread at the back. Hold this tail carefully and make sure that your first four or five stitches secure it. Then trim any excess.

Stitch a series of diagonal bars running from left to right. Then, at the end of the row, return by stitching the top bars from right to left. Drop your needle to the bottom of the next row and repeat the process. Stitches in a sequence interlock, sharing holes with the neighbouring stitch.

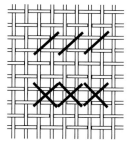

Forming cross-stitches on linen

Forming cross-stitches on Aida

Remember, the number of threads crossed by a single stitch will depend on your fabric: on linen, each stitch covers two threads, on Aida each stitch covers one band of threads. This is shown more clearly in the two diagrams on page 10.

Always work horizontally rather than vertically and do not change directions; even though you may use more embroidery thread the result will look much neater.

Once you have stitched some crosses, use them as your reference point and count from them, rather than from the centre. Your tacked centre lines remain useful as a cross-check that you are counting correctly. Complete each block of colour, jumping short distances where necessary, but always securing the thread at the back by running the needle under existing threads. If blocks are some distance apart, finish off the first and start afresh.

To finish off each section, run your needle through the back of four or five stitches and trim the embroidery thread close to the cloth.

Half-stitch

Many of the charts contain some half-stitches or, as they are sometimes called, three-quarter stitches. These are indicated on the chart by a right-angled triangle and are usually found around the edges of a design. In this case, one diagonal of the cross-stitch is formed in the usual way, but the second stitch is brought down into the central hole of linen, or into the centre of an Aida block.

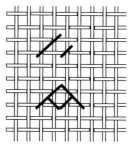

Forming two half-stitches

Where the chart indicates two half-stitches in the same square, you will need to decide which colour should predominate in the second diagonal.

Backstitch

Many of the charts include backstitching to define outlines and provide detail. It is indicated by a solid line on the chart. Backstitch is always worked after cross-stitching is completed and is worked in a continuous line. The method is best described in the diagram below.

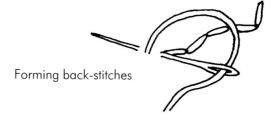

Forming back-stitches

Some Tips

It is important to keep your work as clean and fresh as possible. Don't leave unfinished work in an embroidery hoop for too long as the hoop may mark the fabric. When not in use, always secure the needle at the edge of the fabric to prevent rust marks or thread distortion from spoiling your stitching.

Do not fold work-in-progress; roll it in a layer of tissue paper. A sheet of acetate (available from art supply shops) offers good protection for a large project.

Cut your embroidery thread, as you need it, into 50 cm lengths. Longer strands will start to fray towards the end.

After working a series of stitches, your thread will start to twist. This can give uneven stitches, so occasionally let the needle dangle down from the fabric so that the thread can unwind.

When moving from one area of a colour to another patch of the same colour, don't jump the thread across the back if the gap will remain bare. Such leaps will show through the fabric in the finished work.

If you make an error in counting, do not try to rescue the embroidery thread for reuse. Use a pair of small pointed scissors to snip misplaced stitches and carefully pull out the strands, then stitch correctly with a new piece of embroidery thread.

Avoid the temptation to start or finish off with a knot; it will form a lump when the work is laid flat.

Teaching Children

Cross-stitch is an ideal introduction to needlecraft and the designs in this book may well tempt many boys and girls to take up the craft of cross-stitch and it is important to start them on simple and achievable projects which will not dampen their enthusiasm and deter their interest.

Here are some tips:

- Encourage children to practise the basic cross-stitch by creating coloured patterns on scrap fabric before tackling a design.

- Explain how the key works, making sure they understand that each symbol represents a particular colour.

- Children may like to colour in the key and the chart (you may photocopy a design from the book provided it is for personal use only).

- Choose a large count Aida fabric and a large blunt needle for them to work with.

- Choose a small design which has big blocks of solid colour. Introduce half-stitches only once they have mastered the full cross-stitch.

- Supervise backstitching to begin with. It may be appropriate for you to work the backstitch for younger children.

- Help children make their stitched design into a finished project that they can use or display.

- Help children to chart their own initials, name, or age, using the alphabet and number charts on pages 124-5. If they stitch their name and age on a design, it both personalises it and becomes a milestone in a child's life.

For Baby

There is no limit
to the projects which you can
make to welcome a newborn.
Brighten up a nursery with hand-
made pieces, or stitch an heirloom
which the child will treasure in
years to come. The designs in this
section will never go out of fash-
ion: the Velveteen Rabbit, Tom
Kitten, and Alice's friends from
Wonderland are all classics which
will continue to give pleasure to
each generation.

Alice in Wonderland

Few children's stories have given us as many familiar images and phrases as the works of Lewis Carroll. Alice's Adventures in Wonderland was the extraordinary work of a shy young man whose real name was Charles Dodgson. He was most at ease in the company of girls and his tales were originally created for his favourite child friend, Alice Liddell. When published some years later in 1865, the book was a great success and brought the lecturer in mathematics sufficient fame to gain him an audience with Queen Victoria. Both his first book and Through the Looking Glass, which followed in 1871, were illustrated by John Tenniel, whose images helped to bring life to such ingenious characters as the White Rabbit, Tweedledum and Tweedledee, and the Mad Hatter. The books are also filled with riddles and rhymes and a generous helping of pure nonsense, appealing to the child in each of us.

Scented Sachet

A lavender sachet can help keep a nursery smelling fresh and can double as a holder for safety pins. It's pictured on page 18.

Materials: 14 x 14 cm white linen
with 28 threads per inch;
14 x 14 cm coloured fabric;
polyester stuffing;
dried lavender flowers;
DMC embroidery threads listed.

Stitch count: 43H x 40W

Directions: Stitch the design on the linen. Zigzag the edges of the linen and the backing fabric. Place the two pieces together with right sides facing and sew a 1 cm seam, leaving a gap for turning. Turn the sachet right side out. Push a teaspoon of dried lavender into a handful of polyester stuffing and then fill the sachet with this. Neatly handsew the opening closed. Decorate with a ribbon.

KEY for Alice		
DMC	Colour	Stitches
U 351	red	11
+ 472	green	235
O 793	dark blue	81
■ 841	brown	35
L 842	pale brown	73
− 948	pale peach	110
X 3747	blue	254
✳ 3820	gold	39
•	white	206
Backstitch		
351	red	mouth
317	grey	other details

Bookmark

The White Rabbit checks his timepiece on this bookmark, a delightful gift for a child who will one day grow up to enjoy books.

Materials: 24 x 14 cm white Aida fabric with 18 thread groups per inch; DMC embroidery threads listed.

Stitch count: 111H x 32W

Directions: Align the Aida fabric so that a 14-cm edge is along the top and then stitch the design in the centre.

Press two vertical folds in the fabric, three squares from each side of the design, to create a strip 153 mm wide. Fold the edges under at the centre back where they meet and press. Handsew neatly along the seam.

With a needle or an unpicker, tease out threads at the top and base to form a 15 mm fringe. If you wish to, secure the ends with small, neat overstitches.

	KEY for White Rabbit		
	DMC	Colour	Stitches
O	340	blue	44
X	341	pale blue	268
<	352	peach	33
−	353	pale peach	34
Z	453	pale grey	106
U	907	green	19
*	3820	gold	87
+	3823	cream	54
•		white	457
	317	dark grey	backstitch

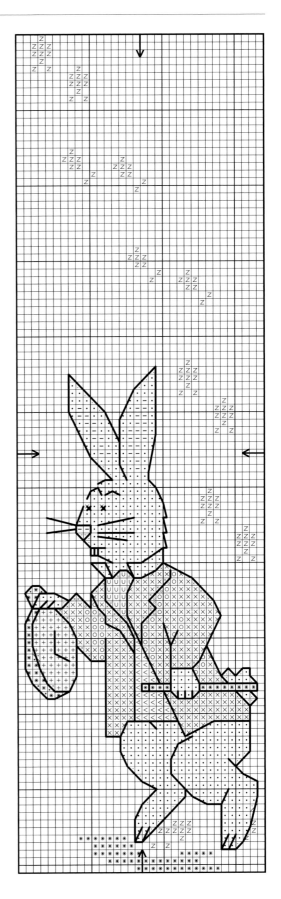

Egg Cosy

An egg cup is a traditional gift to welcome a baby; a cosy featuring Humpty Dumpty makes it that much more charming! The project is shown on page 22.

Materials: 12 x 10 cm white Aida fabric with 14 thread groups per inch; 12 x 20 cm white lining fabric; 12 x 10 cm coloured fabric; DMC embroidery threads listed.

Stitch count: 39H x 30W

Directions: Stitch the design on the Aida fabric. Cut two 12 x 10 cm pieces of lining fabric and a matching piece of coloured cotton. Lay the embroidery on the backing,

right sides facing, and tack an arc around Humpty Dumpty, leaving the base unstitched. Sew, using the tacking as a guide. Trim the edges and zigzag to prevent fraying. Turn the cosy right side out.

Lay the two lining pieces together, then lay the outside section on top and mark an arc around it. Sew the lining pieces together a few mm inside of the marked arc, leaving the base unsewn. Trim the edge and zigzag.

Place the lining section inside the cosy. Turn the edges of both sections in and neatly handsew the lining onto the outer section.

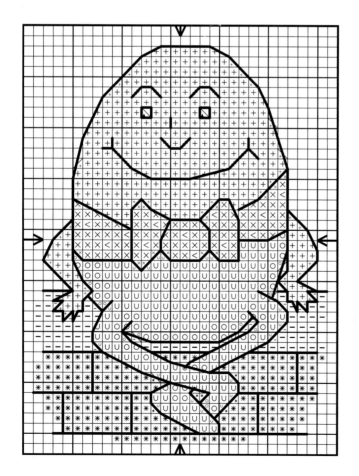

KEY for Humpty Dumpty

	DMC	Colour	Stitches
▲	317	grey	2
X	341	blue	96
<	352	peach	12
–	676	gold	74
+	746	cream	333
O	907	green	66
U	3819	light green	181
*	3827	orange	182
	317	dark grey	backstitch

Baby's Vest

There's no need to restrict your cross-stitching to evenweave fabrics when you can use waste canvas. On page 22, the Cheshire Cat grins his special grin on a baby's garment.

Materials: 10 x 12 cm waste canvas with
14 thread groups per inch;
a baby's vest or jumpsuit;
DMC embroidery threads listed.

Stitch count: 28H x 43W

Directions: Position the waste canvas on the front of the garment, ensuring that it is squared up. Tack around the edges and diagonally so that the canvas is securely attached.

   Stitch the design, using two strands of embroidery thread. When stitching is complete, remove the tacking threads, dampen the canvas with a cloth and slowly pull out the strands of the waste canvas. Carefully press the finished garment.

KEY for Cheshire Cat			
	DMC	Colour	Stitches
✕	754	peach	34
−	782	tan	148
✳	844	dark grey	2
▲	3819	green	16
+	3820	gold	600
○	3826	brown	111
	844	dark grey	backstitch

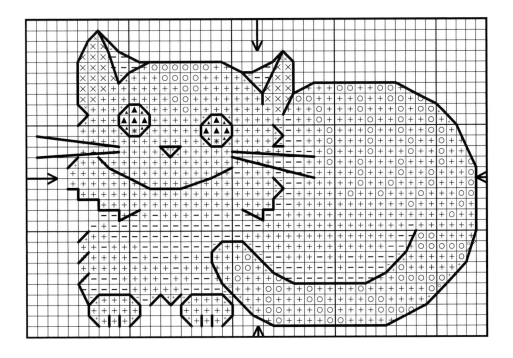

Stitching instructions for
Humpty Dumpty and the
Cheshire Cat can be found
on pages 20-21.

The Mad Hatter's tea-set will
give baby something bright to
look at. Instructions appear on
page 24.

Cot Set

The cot string and hanging toy, shown on page 23, were inspired by the Mad Hatter's tea-party. Measure the width of your cot and cut ribbons to suit.

Materials: 12 x 45 cm white Aida fabric with 11 thread groups per inch; 12 x 45 cm coloured fabric; polyester stuffing; coloured ribbons; DMC embroidery threads listed.

Stitch count: 19H x 32W - teacup
27H x 42W - teapot

Directions: For the cot string, cut three 12 x 10 cm pieces of Aida and stitch a teacup on each one. Cut three pieces of backing fabric and lay each stitched section face down on a backing piece.

Lay two short lengths of ribbon between a pair of fabric pieces, so that the raw edges of the ribbon align with the fabric edges at one side. Tack around the cup, leaving a gap at the other side for turning. Sew along the tacking lines. Trim the edges and turn the section right side out. Repeat with another cup section. On the third section, attach longer ribbons.

Fill each cup with polyester stuffing. Position the loose ends of the short ribbons in the opening of two cup sections and handsew the openings closed. In the remaining opening, secure longer ribbons, matching the other end.

For the hanging toy, cut a 15 x 12 cm piece of Aida and stitch the teapot design in the centre. Cut a matching piece of backing fabric. Lay the cross-stitching on the coloured backing, right sides facing. Tack around the teapot, leaving a gap at the top for turning. Sew, using the tacking as a guide. Trim the edges, turn right side out and fill the toy with polyester stuffing. Position a loop of ribbon between the pieces at the opening, then handsew the opening closed, securing the ribbon loop. Add a ribbon bow.

KEY for Tea-set			
	DMC	Colour	Stitches
X	341	light blue	347
✱	352	peach	132
Z	353	pink	328
L	472	light green	327
+	742	orange	178
–	743	yellow	535
U	907	green	122
O	3807	blue	124
•		white	35
	317	grey	backstitch

The Velveteen Rabbit

In 1920, Margery Williams penned the enchanting story of The Velveteen Rabbit, *the tale of a toy rabbit who starts his life as a Christmas gift to a young boy. The book was subtitled 'Or How Toys Become Real', a state to which the toy rabbit aspires. He is befriended by the Skin Horse, an older and wiser occupant of the toy cupboard, who explains that only a child's love can make a toy real. As the years pass, the Velveteen Rabbit's fur loses its sheen, his thread whiskers fall out, and he is finally discarded after the boy suffers a bout of scarlet fever. It's then that a fairy rewards him for his years of faithful toy service by changing him into a real rabbit, free to play in the fields and meadows. This delightful story has been enjoyed by children of several generations and has become a classic over time.*

Christmas Stocking

This Christmas stocking, shown on page 27, will no doubt be treasured over the years. Personalise it with a child's name on the band.

Materials: 41 x 45 cm of green linen
with 25 threads per inch;
red bias binding;
DMC embroidery threads listed.

Stitch count: 105H x 67W

Directions: Enlarge the stocking pattern by 350%, using a photocopying machine or by rescaling it on graph paper. Fold the Aida fabric in two and pin the pattern on top, then cut out the shape to give you two matching pieces. Zigzag the edges to prevent fraying.

Stitch the design in the lower section of one piece (as in the picture on page 27). Carefully press the finished work.

Lay the two sections of stocking together with the design facing up and sew red bias binding around the sides and foot of the stocking. Finish the opening with another piece of bias binding. Turn the top over to form a collar and stitch a name on the front, if desired. Stitch another piece of bias binding around the opening, over the fold.

KEY for Stocking			
	DMC	Colour	Stitches
O	321	cherry	70
Z	436	light tan	509
■	535	charcoal	2
↑	640	brown	385
<	642	light brown	157
▲	703	green	966
−	712	cream	64
=	725	yellow	113
T	754	pink	56
*	798	blue	67
X	817	red	870
U	904	dark green	64
•		white	92
Backstitch			
	310	black	face
	725	yellow	present tie
	535	grey	other details

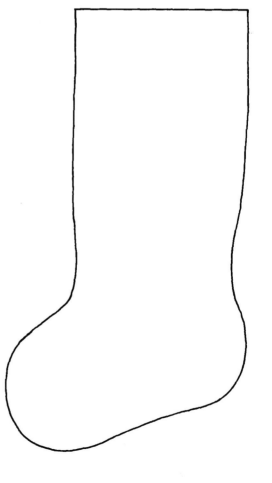

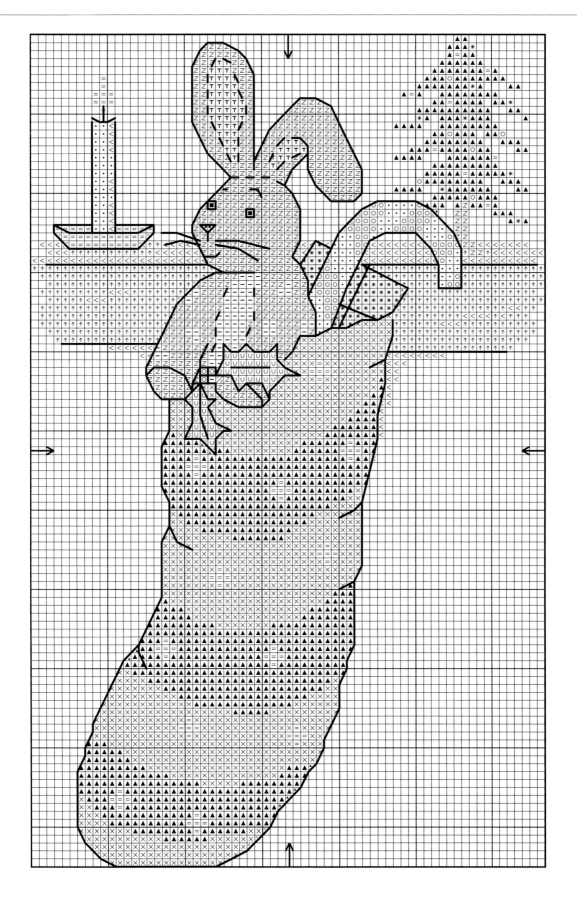

This towel trim depicts the
Velveteen Rabbit as it changes
from a toy into a real rabbit.
The chart is on page 32.

Decorate a bib with a classic
design of the Skin Horse and
other toys. Instructions appear
on page 33.

Towel Trim

In four simple images, the Velveteen Rabbit is transformed from soft toy to bouncy rabbit. It is pictured on page 30.

Materials: A handtowel;
a length of cream Aida band
with 16 thread groups per inch;
DMC embroidery threads listed.

Stitch count: 24H (width is adaptable)

Directions: Cut a strip of Aida band 4 cm wider than the width of the towel and stitch the figures onto it so that they are evenly

	KEY for Velveteen Rabbit		
	DMC	Colour	Stitches
X	436	light tan	703
−	471	green	84
O	535	dark grey	4
=	712	cream	80
■	754	pink	27
·		white	23
	535	dark grey	backstitch

spaced. Tack the strip onto your towel and then slipstitch along the edges, turning the ends under neatly. Press the towel carefully to complete.

Feeding Bib

A picture of this charming item is on page 31.

Materials: 25 x 30 cm cream Aida fabric
with 14 thread groups per inch;
25 x 30 cm white fabric;
2 m green bias binding;
DMC embroidery threads listed.

Stitch count: 54H x 66W

Directions: Draw the 23 x 28 cm bib
shape on paper, using the pattern on page
126 as a guide. Make sure the neck is large
enough to fit the baby comfortably. Mark the
shape onto the Aida and stitch the design in
the lower half of the fabric.

Cut the Aida and lining fabric to shape.
Zigzag the fabric edges together. Trim the
outside edges with bias binding. Pin a 1 m
strip of bias binding around the neckline so
that the ties are of even length. Starting at
one tie end, sew the bias binding edges
together, continue sewing around the neckline and up to the end of the other tie.

KEY for Horse & Toys			
	DMC	Colour	Stitches
−	317	grey	20
O	350	red	243
T	353	pink	28
∧	434	brown	42
Z	436	light tan	682
■	535	dark grey	3
U	702	green	74
+	704	light green	41
•	739	beige	197
X	817	dark red	109
	535	dark grey	backstitch

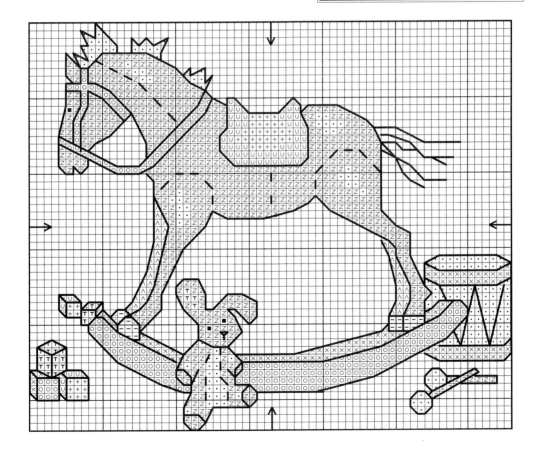

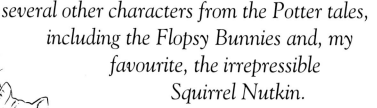 Tom Kitten

In the years following the publication of The Tale of Peter Rabbit, *its author Beatrix Potter earned enough money from this bestseller to purchase a farm in the Lake District. Her precious Hill Top farm became the setting for* The Tale of Tom Kitten *which was published in 1907 and one of the locals, a kitten nicknamed Pickles because of its tendency to get into them, became the model for the endearing hero. Tom, like many of Beatrix's best creations, is rather naughty and quite unable to keep his clothes clean or buttoned. He reappeared in another book,* The Tale of Samuel Whiskers, *where he narrowly escapes becoming pudding for a pair of acquisitive rats. This chapter also draws upon several other characters from the Potter tales, including the Flopsy Bunnies and, my favourite, the irrepressible Squirrel Nutkin.*

Copyright © Frederick Warne & Co, 1998

Soft Toy

Tom Kitten, in typical disarray, makes a delightful toy, shown on the previous page. Add a small bell into the stuffing so that he jingles to entertain baby.

Materials: 21 x 15 cm white Aida fabric with 14 thread groups per inch; 21 x 15 cm backing fabric; polyester stuffing; a small bell; DMC embroidery threads listed.

Stitch count: 86H x 55W

Directions: Stitch the design on the Aida fabric and carefully press the finished work. Trim around the design, allowing a 2 cm margin, and zigzag to secure edges. Trim and zigzag backing fabric to match. Lay the two together with right sides facing and sew around the design, allowing a 1 cm seam, and leaving a gap of several centimetres.

Wrap some polyester stuffing around a small bell. Turn the toy right side out and fill it with polyester stuffing. Handsew the gap closed, making sure that no stuffing can be pulled out.

	KEY for Tom Kitten		
	DMC	Colour	Stitches
ㄱ	437	light brown	252
O	472	green	556
✳	611	brown	474
−	739	sand	151
•	775	light blue	166
+	809	dark blue	585
×	3021	dark brown	602
U	3325	blue	690
	3021	dark brown	backst.

Copyright © Frederick Warne & Co, 1998

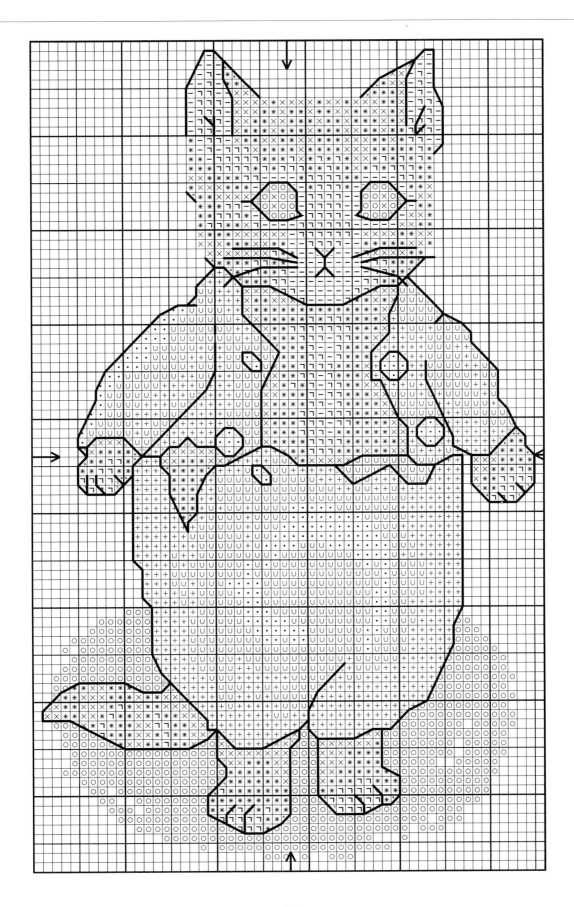

Birth Notice

The endpapers of Beatrix Potter's books featured a variety of charming illustrations. This design is adapted from one of these; the noticeboard originally listed all her titles. The main chart appears overleaf; the alphabet chart is on page 124.

Materials: 40 x 48 cm white linen with 28 threads per inch; white board or heavy card; DMC embroidery threads listed.

Stitch count: 108H x 158W

Directions: Stitch the design in the centre of the fabric, including the child's name and date of birth. Press the work carefully. Cut strong white board to a suitable size. Lay the work over the board and make sure that it is centred. Fold the edges of the fabric around the board and use a strong thread to lace the edges together– side to side and top to bottom.

Fit the covered board into a ready-made frame or have it professionally framed.

	DMC	Colour	Stitches
		KEY for Birth Notice	
S	351	peach	148
X	352	pale peach	634
O	353	pale pink	188
U	437	light brown	415
⌐	471	green	432
◆	472	light green	725
＼	504	mint green	196
H	597	teal	220
<	640	dark fawn	92
N	642	fawn	51
■	646	grey	154
–	648	pale grey	268
+	712	cream	359
↑	738	sand	868
Z	828	pale blue	352
▲	840	dark brown	83
I	841	brown	310
●	842	light brown	260
→	932	blue	90
∩	976	dark tan	34
I	977	tan	205
‰	3041	purple	91
=	3042	light purple	196
·		white	246
	413	dark grey	backstitch

	DMC	Colour	Stitches
<	472	pale green	87
+	642	fawn	491
X	646	dark fawn	300
·	712	cream	70
✳	840	brown	22
Z	976	dark tan	179
U	977	tan	263
−	3053	green	129
O	3827	light tan	152
	413	dark grey	backstitch

KEY for Squirrel Nutkin

Tissue Box

Squirrel Nutkin and his brother Twinkleberry gather nuts on a cover to fit over a tissue box.

Materials: cream Aida fabric
with 16 thread groups per inch;
sturdy cardboard;
tape;
DMC embroidery threads listed.

Stitch count: 60H x 50W

Directions: Wrap a tape measure around the tissue box to be covered and cut Aida 2 cm longer than the perimeter, and 2 cm more than the box's height. Stitch the design on the Aida so that it will lie in the centre of a panel. Cut four pieces of sturdy cardboard

slightly larger than the four sides of the tissue box. Lay the stitched work face down and arrange the pieces of cardboard on the back, with a gap of 2 mm between each one. Tape down the top and bottom edges of the fabric onto the back of the card.

Wrap the covered side section around the tissue box and tape the ends together, then slipstitch the edges together. Cut card to fit on the top with a hole in the centre to remove tissues. Cover this lid with Aida, taping down the loose edges at the back. For the centre hole, cut a number of small flaps in the fabric and tape these at the back around the hole. Handsew the lid onto the box base.

Nappy Holder

The Flopsy Bunnies feature on this handy item, which is shown on page 43.

Materials: 20 x 40 cm coloured linen with 28 threads per inch; 76.5 x 112 cm plain fabric; a wooden coathanger; cardboard; ribbon; DMC embroidery threads listed.

Stitch count: 49H x 94W

Directions: Lay the coathanger on paper and mark around it, allowing an extra 1 cm at the top and sides and 15 cm below it. Use this paper template to cut a piece of coloured linen (28 count) and a piece of plain fabric. Zigzag the edges of the linen to prevent fraying and then stitch the design in the centre. The background green is stitched with a single strand of thread.

Lay the shaped pieces together, right sides facing, and sew a seam around the top and sides, leaving a 1 cm gap at the top centre. Turn the section right side out and thread the coathanger hook through the hole.

From the remaining plain fabric, cut two base rectangles of 36 x 26.5 cm and the main piece measuring 112 x 50 cm. Hem both short edges of the main piece. With right

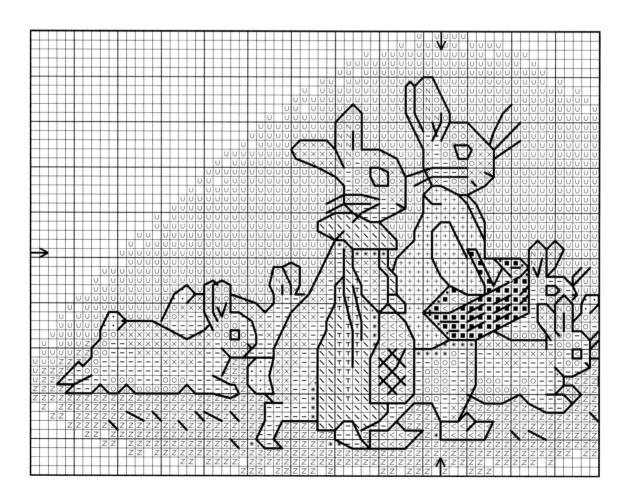

Copyright © Frederick Warne & Co, 1998

sides facing, pin one of its long edges around a base piece, so that there is a central opening for the nappies. Sew to secure and then turn right side out.

Sew a running stitch along the raw top edge and gather it to fit the opening of the coathanger section. Turn the edges of the opening under neatly, pin the main section in position and sew to secure.

Cut a 31 x 22 cm piece of strong cardboard and cover it with the remaining fabric rectangle, taping down or gluing the loose edges at the back. Place this, fabric side up, in the bottom of the nappy holder.

	KEY for Flopsy Family		
	DMC	Colour	Stitches
✱	414	grey	30
×	437	light tan	294
■	729	tan	60
–	738	sand	368
O	739	cream	231
+	760	rose	117
U	772	light green	1212
\	813	blue	96
T	827	pale blue	30
<	840	brown	87
N	948	peach	27
Z	3348	green	622
•		white	36
	413	dark grey	backstitch

Early
Years

Life at this stage is pretty
exciting with lots of things to learn
and do. To help toddlers through,
Ned the donkey introduces the
concept of numbers. Maisy and
Elmer are two new companions
from the world of picture books,
while Noddy is a familiar face to
many of us. The designs in this
section are packed with primary
colours and sure to catch the eye
of every toddler, no matter what
else they're busy doing.

Ned

There aren't that many donkeys in children's literature. There are even fewer green donkeys, and only one of them is called Ned. Ned's first appearance in a picture book was in a cameo role in Maybe It's a Pirate. He almost stole the show and so starred next in a book titled, of course, Ned. This delightful story tells of young Emily who is apprehensive about starting school and is not keen to leave her donkey behind. She soon discovers that school is great fun and that Ned is better off at home, guarding her bedroom from dragons. Ned is not as well known as some book characters, but he is dear to the heart of many. He was adopted by London's Great Ormond Street Hospital for Sick Children as their mascot and money from every sale of his book was donated to the hospital for some time. Ned is now being set to work again by his creator Selina Young and is due to appear in another picture book, along with four little books.

Ned ™ © Selina Young 1993

Counting Sampler

In this attractive design, Ned introduces toddlers to the first ten numbers using items commonly found in the class. The finished work appears on page 50.

Materials: 55 x 55 cm white Aida fabric with 11 thread bands per inch; white board or heavy card stock; DMC embroidery threads listed.

Stitch count: 160H x 160W

Directions: Note that the design appears over this page and pages 51-53, with the key on page 51. Stitch the design in the centre of the fabric and press the work carefully.

To back the work, cut strong white board to a suitable size. Lay the work over the board and make sure that it is centred. Fold the edges of the fabric around the board and use a strong thread to lace the edges together, side to side and top to bottom. Fit the covered board into a ready-made frame or have it professionally framed.

KEY for Ned and numbers

	DMC	Colour	Stitches		DMC	Colour	Stitches
=	310	black	4	X	798	blue	886
I	341	pale blue	1487	\	806	teal	236
U	351	dark pink	289	O	817	dark red	294
˥	352	pink	459	I	921	brown	160
T	642	mushroom	157	N	973	yellow	523
+	666	red	543	●	3607	purple	370
Z	676	light brown	175	→	3609	light purple	384
✳	699	dark green	313	S	3766	aqua	388
↑	701	green	760	·		white	186
∩	722	orange	740				
−	742	gold	297		310	black	backstitch

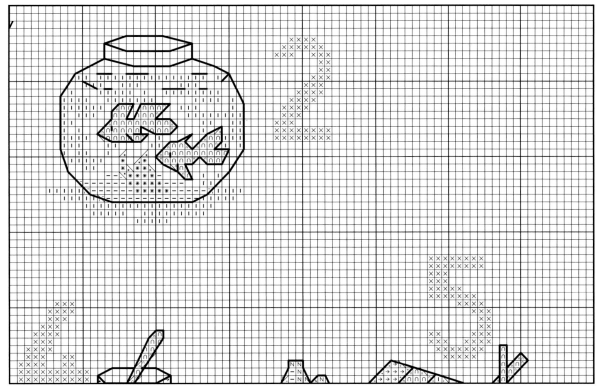

51

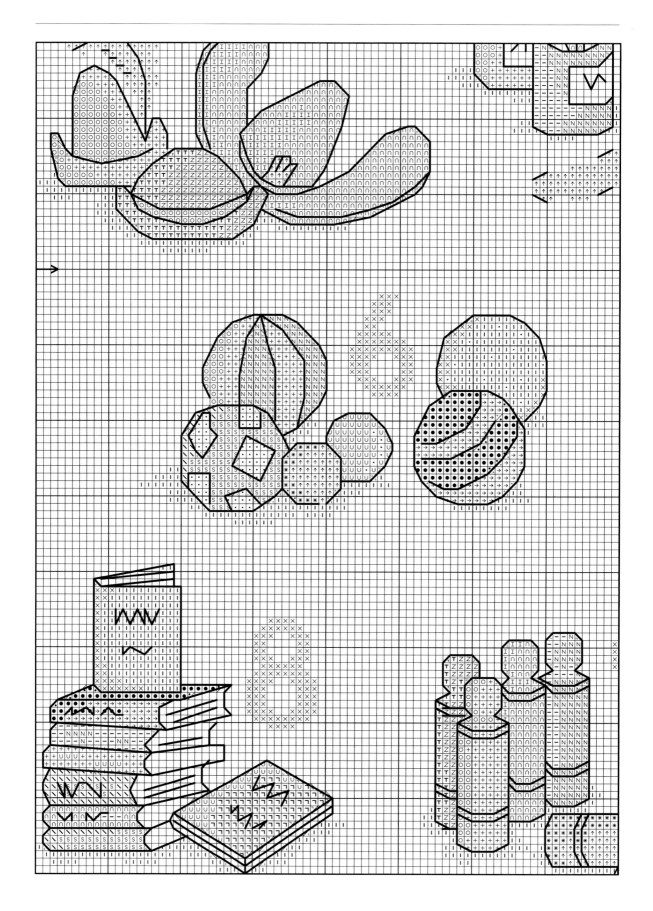

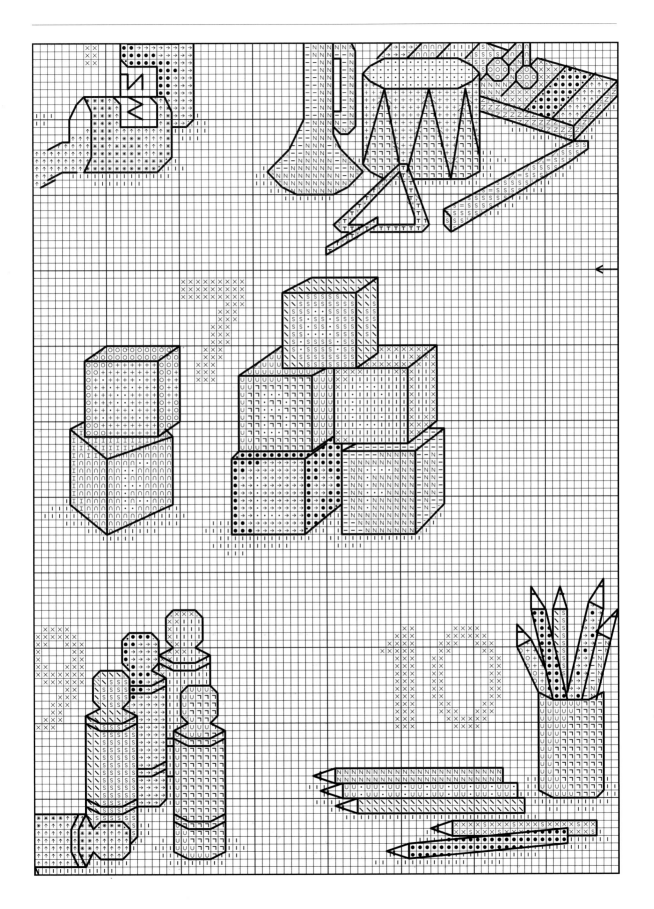

Maisy

Everyone is crazy for Maisy the mouse! This is no retiring rodent: she's a lively character who goes about the business of being a mouse-toddler with great verve and humour. The books in which Maisy stars are not so much stories as snapshots of a child's world—going to playschool, to the playground or getting ready for bed—and are filled with items which young children love to identify. They are, moreover, novelty books in which flaps lift and tabs pull to reveal a flea beneath an elephant's ear or to make a turtle play the ukelele. Maisy's creator, Lucy Cousins, has produced a number of bright and instructive books, with and without our heroine. Recently, she has given the mouse a house in an amazing book with rooms that pop up and press-out pieces that simply demand to be played with. Lucy has young children of her own, which helps to explain her uncanny ability to catch the eyes and capture the hearts of small people.

Maisy ™
© 1990 Lucy Cousins
Licensed by Copyrights

Dungarees

This design, featuring Maisy on her tricycle, adds charm to a pair of plain dungarees on page 54.

Materials: 20 x 20 cm white Aida fabric
with 14 thread groups per inch;
white lining fabric;
dungarees;
coloured bias binding;
DMC embroidery threads listed.

Stitch count: 50H x 38W

Directions: Stitch the design on the Aida. The backstitch is worked with two strands, except for the whiskers, which are stitched with three stands.

Cut the fabric to the size of the desired patch and line it with white fabric. Lay bias binding around the patch and fold it over to conceal the raw fabric edges. Sew around the binding, securing all layers. Pin the patch on the garment and sew in place. To make a pocket, sew only three sides onto the garment.

	KEY for both Maisy charts		
	DMC	Colour	Stitches
■	310	black	438
O	350	red	185
+	754	peach	198
−	798	blue	27
▲	912	green	180
×	972	yellow	5
•		white	160
Backstitch			
	754	peach	whiskers
	310	black	other details

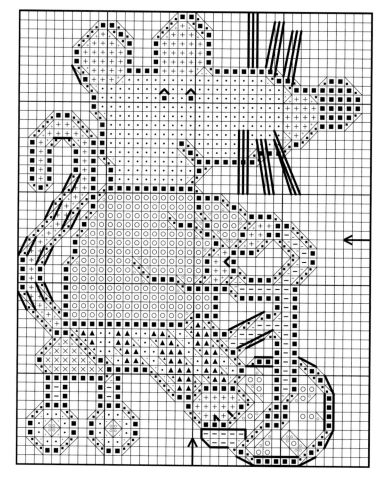

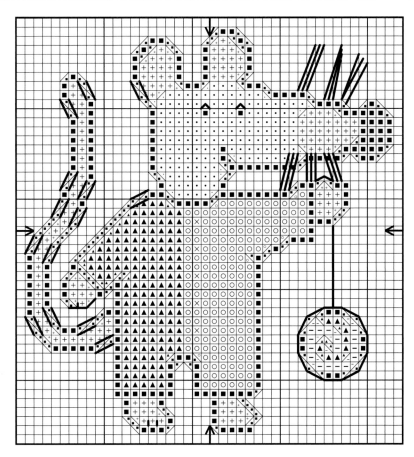

Purse

This purse, shown on page 54, could also be used as a bag for that precious yo-yo.

Materials: 15 x 15 cm white Aida fabric
with 14 thread groups per inch;
white lining fabric;
coloured fabric;
bias binding;
coloured cord;
DMC embroidery threads listed.

Stitch count: 45H x 42W

Directions: Follow the instructions on page 84 to make a 12 cm square patch featuring the above design. The backstitch is worked with two strands, save for the whiskers, which are worked with three strands.

To make the bag or purse, cut two 15 x 19 cm pieces of coloured fabric. Lay these sections together with right sides facing and sew a 1 cm seam around three edges, leaving one short edge unsewn. Turn this edge over twice and sew a hem, 1 cm deep.

Cut a suitable length of cord and dip each end in white glue to prevent fraying. Sew each end securely along one side of the bag. Turn the bag right side out. Sew a large button onto the front of the bag, near the opening. On the opposite side, form a loop of embroidery thread and strengthen it with a series of buttonhole stitches.

Stitch the cross-stitched patch onto the front of the purse.

Music Picture

Maisy and her friends make music in a vibrant picture parade on pages 58-9. The animals could be stitched individually on smaller items.

Materials: 50 x 30 cm white Aida fabric with 11 thread groups per inch; sturdy white card; acrylic paints; DMC embroidery threads listed.

Stitch count: 46H x 138W

Directions: Zigzag the fabric edges to prevent fraying and then stitch the design in the centre. The backstitch is worked with two strands, except for the whiskers which are stitched with three strands and the ukelele strings which are stitched with a single strand. Carefully press the work.

Cut a 35 x 15 cm piece of stiff card and position the embroidery over it, making sure it is straight. Fold the edges of the fabric over and tape or pin them down at the back. Lace the top and bottom edges with strong thread. Repeat this with the two side edges.

Cut a 45 x 25 cm card as a backing panel. Mark a 5 cm border around the edges and paint this in blocks of bright colours using acrylic paints. When the paint is dry, glue or otherwise fix the embroidery panel onto the backing panel. Attach a length of string on the back for hanging.

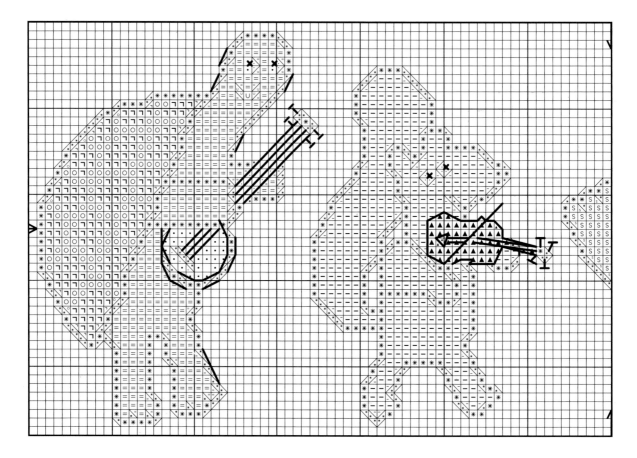

	DMC	Colour	Stitches
✳	310	black	1325
U	350	red	39
–	433	brown	419
▲	436	tan	48
O	502	teal	110
✕	754	peach	181
<	798	blue	138
⌐	909	dark green	173
=	912	light green	313
+	928	grey	103
N	970	orange	65
S	972	yellow	433
4	3803	purple	66
•		white	206

KEY for Maisy's musical friends

Backstitch

754	peach	whiskers
502	teal	ukelele strings
928	grey	violin strings
310	black	other details

Maisy ™
© 1992 Lucy Cousins
Licensed by Copyrights

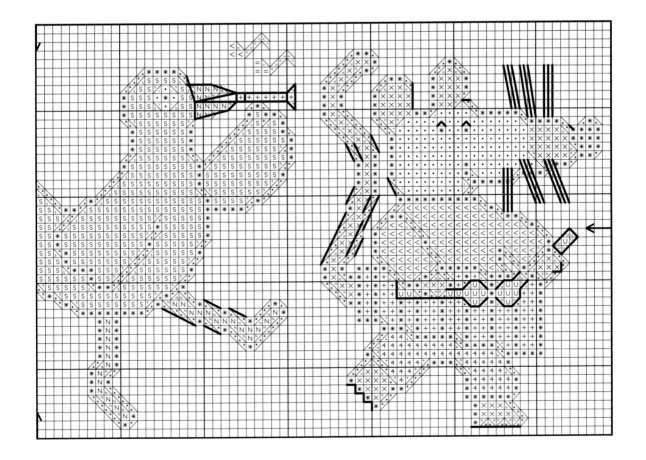

Noddy

Enid Blyton wrote a phenomenal number of books for children of different ages but her most enduring creation was Noddy, the young toy with a tendency to wobble his head. The first of twenty-four Noddy books was published in 1949 and since then his escapades have been translated into over twenty languages. In France, Noddy is known as Oui Oui, in Iceland he is Doddi, and in Germany he goes under the name of Purzelknirps. Noddy lives in Toyland, along with a multitude of other characters such as Tessie Bear, Mr Plod and, of course, his best friend Big-Ears the brownie. His pride and joy is his little car and he can usually be seen around Toy Town, giving other toys a lift somewhere. Noddy, easily identified by the large bell on the end of his cap, now has his own television series and continues to delight children everywhere with his adventures.

Noddy ™
© Enid Blyton Ltd. All Rights reserved.

Travel Bag

Noddy and Big-Ears make good companions on a long journey. Stitch them on a bag for holding books and small toys, pictured on page 62.

Materials: 56 x 27 cm cream Aida fabric with 14 thread groups per inch; 56 x 27 cm white lining fabric; coloured cloth tape; DMC embroidery threads listed.

Stitch count: 76H x 69W

Directions: Fold the linen fabric in half to form a 28 x 27 cm rectangle. Stitch the design 45 mm up from the folded base. Press the work carefully.

Fold the fabric in half, right sides facing. Sew a 1 cm seam down each side. Turn over and sew a 2 cm hem around the opening of the bag.

Cut two 25 cm lengths of strong cloth tape. Pin the ends onto the Aida hem to form a handle on each side. Sew the tape ends securely in place. Turn the bag right side out.

Fold the white lining fabric in half and seam the sides to form a matching bag. Insert the lining bag, wrong side out, into the Aida bag. Turn in the raw edge of the lining bag and slipstitch it neatly onto the Aida.

KEY for Noddy & Big-Ears			
	DMC	Colour	Stitches
✳	310	black	21
4	340	purple	137
Z	648	grey	410
−	666	red	762
■	701	green	8
N	797	dark blue	138
U	798	blue	190
T	947	orange	18
O	951	peach	369
X	973	yellow	369
▲	3325	pale blue	12
+	3747	mauve	209
<	3776	brown	47
·		white	1142
Backstitch			
	666	red	kerchief
	310	black	other details

	KEY for Noddy		
	DMC	Colour	Stitches
✱	310	black	2
–	666	red	324
N	701	green	41
<	740	orange	114
U	798	blue	246
O	951	peach	261
⊓	973	yellow	185
✕	3325	pale blue	87
T	3776	brown	53
+		white	23
	310	black	backstitch

Birthday Card

Send a child a special birthday greeting.

Materials: 15 x 11 cm white Aida fabric
with 16 thread groups per inch;
17 x 37.5 cm coloured card;
double-sided tape; ribbon;
DMC embroidery threads listed.

Stitch count: 64H x 40W

Directions: Stitch the design on the Aida. Lightly score two lines on the card with a knife and fold, creating three even panels. Trim a narrow strip off the left panel. Cut a 8 x 11.5 cm window in the centre panel with a sharp knife. Apply double-sided tape on the inside of the centre panel, position the stitched work, and stick down the left-hand panel as a backing. Decorate with a ribbon.

Finger Puppets

With puppets of Noddy, Big-Ears, Tessie Bear, Mr Plod, Sly and Mr Wobbly Man, children can recreate Toyland adventures. They are pictured on page 70.

Materials: 12.5 x 50 cm white Aida fabric with 14 thread groups per inch; 25 x 50 cm white lining fabric; 12.5 x 50 cm coloured fabric; DMC embroidery threads listed.

Stitch count: approximately 45H x 30W

Directions: Stitch each design on Aida fabric, allowing plenty of space between the figures. For each puppet, cut two 12 x 8 cm pieces of lining fabric and one of coloured fabric. Separate the figures, lay each one face down on a lining piece and sew along the base, 5 mm below the bottom row of cross-stitches. Trim the edge and zigzag it, then turn the piece inside out so that the design faces out and is backed with the white fabric. Tack 5 mm around the figure, stitching the layers together.

Sew the other lining piece and the coloured piece together along one side, forming the base. Trim the edge and zigzag, then turn the piece inside out. Place the two sections together with the bases aligned and with the cross-stitching and coloured fabric facing each other. Sew them together, using the basted outline as a guide. Trim the edges and zigzag to secure threads. Turn the puppet inside out.

To make a puppet stand, drill holes in a narrow block of timber and glue in short sections of dowel.

	DMC	Colour	Stitches
↑	307	yellow	288
■	310	black	81
O	356	rust	157
⌐	550	purple	25
U	598	aqua	76
+	666	red	370
<	704	green	300
N	722	apricot	169
T	744	pale yellow	344
Z	772	pale green	154
X	798	blue	417
\	825	navy blue	498
*	905	dark green	47
▼	921	brown	119
→	947	orange	55
I	951	peach	548
●	973	gold	123
=	996	light blue	30
◆	3325	pale blue	93
∩	3689	pale mauve	220
▲	3820	tan	10
·		white	361

KEY for Toy Town friends

Backstitch

356	rust	waistcoat stars
666	red	Big Ears' kerchief
704	green	trousers, bow tie
310	black	other details

The Toyland Train decorates
a pin board for the bedroom.
Instructions can be found on
page 72.

These Toy Town finger puppets
offer hours of story-making fun.
Instructions for stitching them
are on page 68.

Pin Board

The Toyland train decorates this notice board, pictured on page 71.

Materials: 50 x 55 cm cream linen
with 28 threads per inch;
pin board;
tape or a staple gun;
DMC embroidery threads listed.

Stitch count: 44H x 198W

Directions: Zigzag fabric edges to prevent fraying. Tack a marker thread 15 cm in from a long edge; this marks the base of the train. Stitch the design so that the carriages are in a line (refer to the photograph on page 71) connected by hooks. Press the work.

Cut a 40 x 45 cm piece of pin board (soft chipboard or thick cork) and position the embroidery over it, making sure it is straight. Fold the edges of the fabric over and tape or staple them down at the back.

	KEY for Toyland Train		
	DMC	*Colour*	*Stitches*
■	310	black	49
X	453	pale grey	120
−	550	purple	19
O	613	beige	107
Z	666	red	713
⌐	704	green	9
▼	722	apricot	1160
U	744	pale yellow	151
+	798	blue	322
N	825	navy	140
4	921	brown	45
↑	951	peach	409
\	973	gold	87
▲	992	turquoise	62
S	3325	pale blue	16
T	3340	orange	37
I	3689	pale mauve	128
●	3820	pale tan	363
·		white	175

Backstitch
666	red	Big Ears' kerchief
704	green	Mr Wobbly's tie
310	black	other details

Elmer

Elmer the multicoloured elephant has made a dramatic impression since David McKee let him loose in the world of children's books. Children love him because his bright patchwork hide has a hand-coloured quality and his squares sometimes change colour, making him just that bit unpredictable. Now the star of various adventure stories, bath time books, board books and even a pop-up book, Elmer is quite an individual (in both appearance and personality) with a cheeky sense of fun and a penchant for playing practical jokes on his friends. He lives in a beautiful landscape of lush jungles and open plains filled with exotic plants and a flock of strange blue birds. The adventures and mishaps which he experiences there are enjoyed by children from China to Finland; in Japan there is even a play about him!

Elmer © 1998 David McKee
All rights reserved.

Toy Tidy

The hanging tidy on page 74 encourages children to clean up their toys while playing hide-and-seek with Elmer and his friends.

Materials: 48 x 30 cm grey Aida fabric
with 14 thread groups per inch;
base fabric; lining fabric;
dowel;
coloured bias binding;
DMC embroidery threads listed.

Stitch count: 47H x 62W each figure

Directions: Cut five 15 x 16 cm pieces of the Aida fabric. On four of these, stitch the plain elephants, using two strands of thread for the backstitch. On the fifth piece, stitch Elmer in bright colours, using only one strand for the backstitch.

Back each stitched piece with white lining fabric and tack the sections together around the edges. Lay a piece of bias binding around each section, folding it over so that the raw edges are concealed. Stitch around the bias binding, to create five patches.

Cut a piece of base fabric approximately 55 x 65 cm in size, with a lining fabric to match. Sew the two pieces together by sewing a seam around two long edges and one narrow one. Turn the base section right side out and fold the top edges inside the bag to create a deep seam. Cut three 12 cm lengths of bias binding and fold each one in half. Insert one loop at each end of the opening and the third in the middle. Hand-sew the opening closed, making sure the bias binding loops are quite secure.

Arrange the embroidered patches on the base fabric and pin in place. Secure these in place by sewing around the sides and base of each one to form pockets.

	KEY for Elmer & friends		
	DMC	Colour	Stitches
X	310	black	138
■	317	grey	48
−	318	light grey	35
N	333	purple	268
+	349	red	356
T	702	green	251
Z	721	orange	317
O	973	yellow	258
<	996	blue	207
U	3806	pink	315
•		white	130
Backstitch			
	310	black	eye
	413	dark grey	other details

Cut a 55 cm piece of dowel and paint it. Thread the dowel through the loops and hang the toy tidy from two hooks.

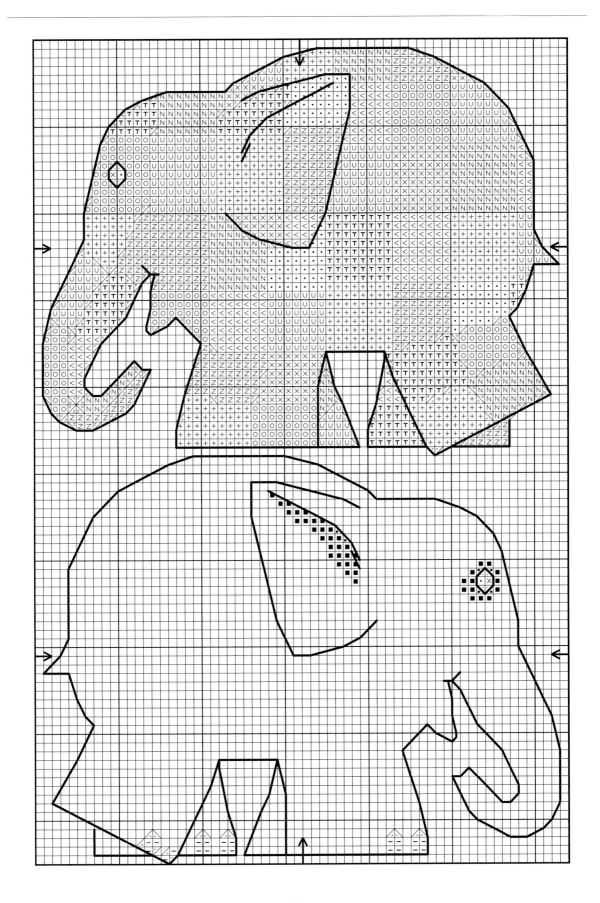

Magnets

Cheer up the door of the refrigerator with magnets, featuring Elmer and his black-and-white cousin Wilbur.

Materials: 30 x 20 cm white Aida fabric with 14 thread groups per inch; white backing fabric; sturdy white card small magnets; DMC embroidery threads listed.

Stitch count: 37H x 41W each figure

Directions: Cut two 15 x 10 cm pieces of Aida fabric. Stitch Elmer on one piece and Wilbur on the other.

To make each magnet, lay a piece of backing fabric on the stitched work, right sides facing. Sew an arc around the design, 5 mm away from the cross-stitching, leaving the base unsewn. Trim the fabric to a 5 mm seam and turn the work right side out.

Cut a piece of white card to a suitable shape and slip it in. Handsew the opening closed. Glue a magnet onto the back.

KEY for Elmer & Wilbur			
	DMC	Colour	Stitches
X	310	black	500
−	333	purple	106
O	349	red	194
+	702	green	137
U	721	orange	116
⊐	973	yellow	119
T	996	blue	120
<	3806	pink	108
•		white	582
	310	black	backstitch

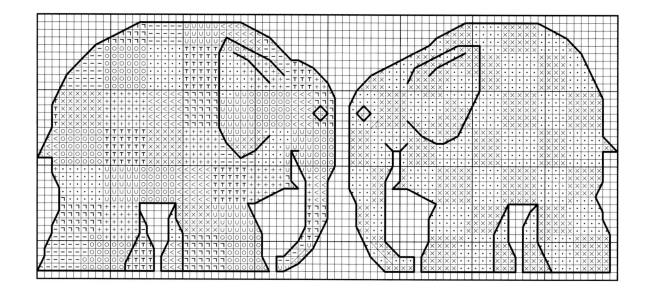

Photo Frame

*An elephant on stilts is not a common sight,
but then Elmer is no common elephant.
Adjust the size of the window to suit the
chosen photograph.*

Materials: 23 x 27 cm coloured linen
with 28 threads per inch;
19 x 23 cm sturdy white card;
double-sided tape;
DMC embroidery threads listed.

Stitch count: 106H x 77W

Directions: Stitch the design on the fabric
and press the finished work carefully.

Trace the oval at the right and transfer it
onto the card so that it is 2 cm from the
bottom edge. Cut out the window with a
sharp knife. Lay double-sided tape around
the oval window and then position the
stitched work over the card.

If you have fray-prevention liquid, apply
a thin line onto the fabric, around the edges
of the window. Snip the fabric in the centre
of the window and then cut towards the
window edges to form darts. Turn the darts
over and tape them neatly onto the back of
the card.

Turn the outside edges of the fabric over
and secure them on the back of the frame
with more tape.

Position a suitable photograph behind the
window and tape it onto the back of the
frame.

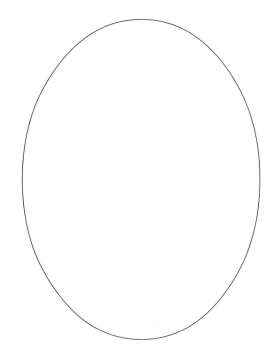

	KEY for Elmer on stilts		
	DMC	Colour	Stitches
X	310	black	187
N	333	purple	226
+	349	red	214
T	702	green	189
Z	721	orange	218
O	973	yellow	251
▲	992	turquoise	466
<	996	blue	109
U	3806	pink	270
•		white	211
	310	black	backstitch

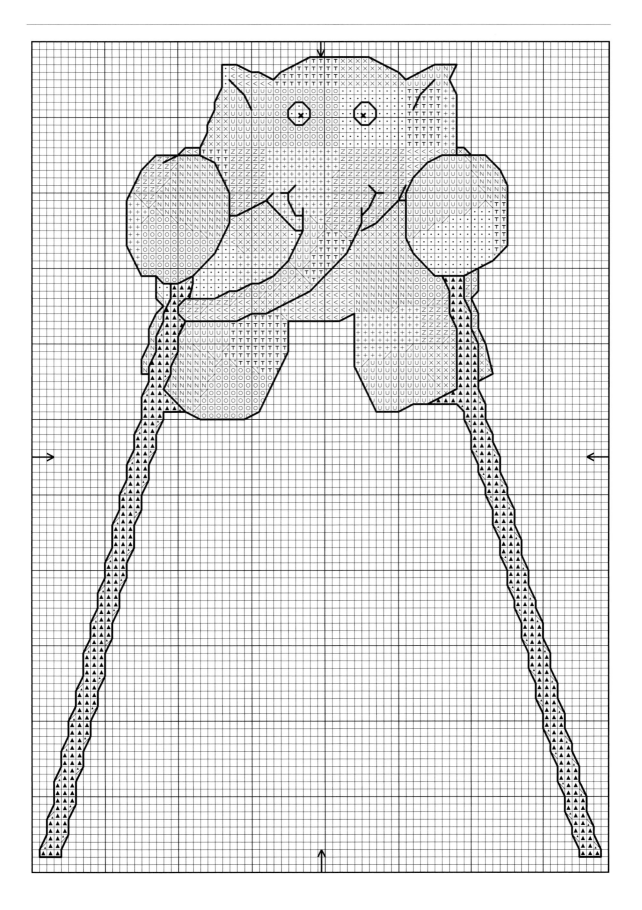

Cushion

A patchwork cushion is the perfect setting for Elmer in his natural environment.

Materials: 25 x 25 cm coloured Aida fabric with 14 thread groups per inch; coloured fabrics; white lining fabric; a cushion pad or filler; DMC embroidery threads listed.

Stitch count: 100H x 90W

Directions: Stitch the design on pages 112-3 in the centre of the Aida fabric. Press the finished work carefully and cut it down to a 22 cm square.

Cut twelve pieces from coloured fabrics, each measuring 12 cm square, and arrange them around the centre panel. Sew the pieces together in stages, allowing seams of 1 cm and pressing the seams as you work. Sew two squares together and then sew this section along one side of the centre panel.

Repeat on the other side. Piece four squares into a long strip, then make another one. Sew these strips along the top and bottom of the panel, to form a single section which should measure 42 cm square. Line this with white fabric.

Cut backing fabric to match the cushion front. Lay the front and back sections together, right sides facing. Sew around three sides, allowing a 1 cm seam. Snip away excess fabric at the corners. Turn the cushion right sides out and press a 1 cm seam at the open edge. Insert the cushion pad or filler and slipstitch the opening closed.

Elmer © 1998 David McKee
All rights reserved.

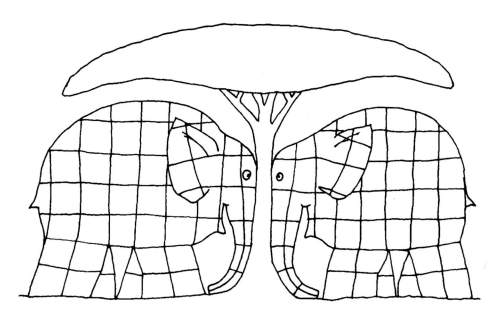

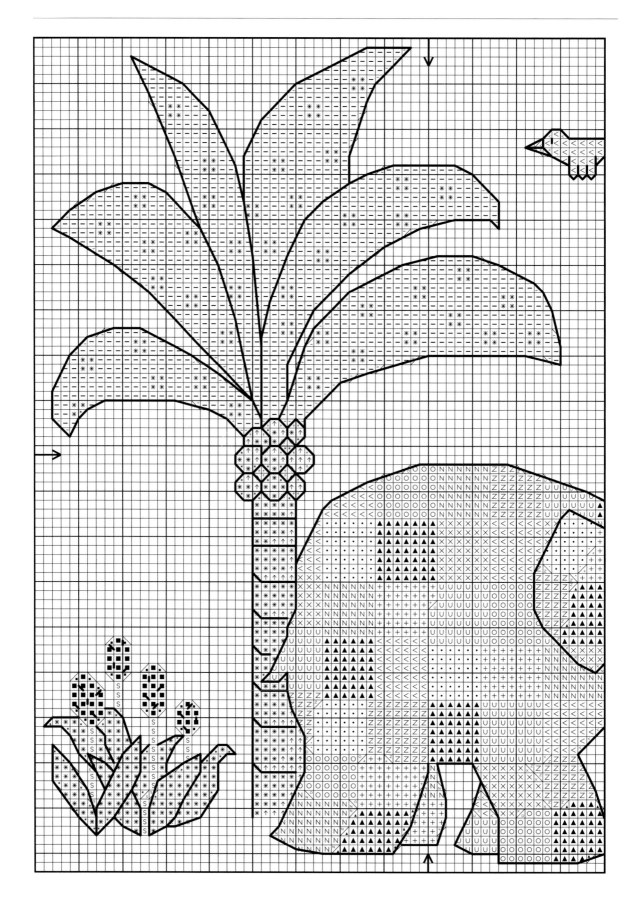

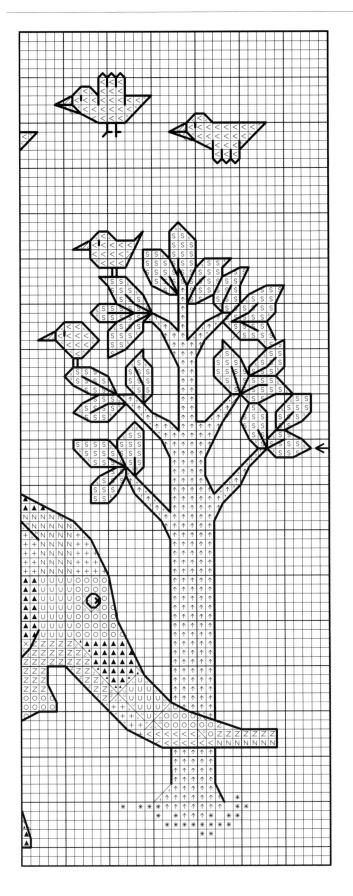

	DMC	Colour	Stitches
X	310	black	110
N	333	purple	201
▲	349	red	294
■	353	peach	67
+	702	dark green	196
−	704	green	1135
Z	721	orange	211
O	973	yellow	203
<	996	blue	304
✳	3348	light green	524
↑	3778	brown	369
U	3806	pink	224
S	3830	rust	336
•		white	153

KEY for Elmer in jungle

Backstitch

310	black	eye, birds
3830	rust	flower heads
413	dark grey	other details

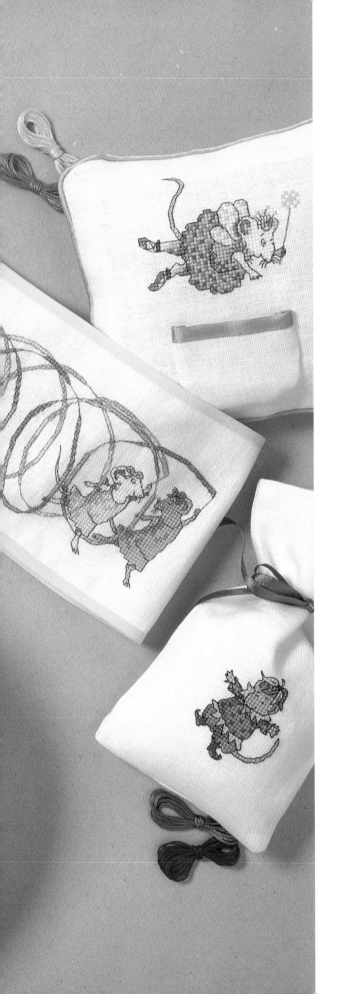

Growing Up

As children grow older, it can become quite difficult to find a gift that pleases both you and them. Here is a collection of friends, both old and new, which will be very acceptable to today's child: Postman Pat, Thomas the Tank Engine, Angelina, plus the delightful Big Bear and Little Bear. They feature on an array of wonderful gifts which will delight everyone, but there's no need to stop there: you can use the designs to decorate clothing, doorplates, and a hundred other things.

Postman Pat

Among the characters in this book, Postman Pat is unique because he started out life as an animated television figure but has since featured in a number of storybooks. Pat is the Postman for Greendale, a picturesque village in the English countryside. He always has a friendly smile and a kind word for all, and is usually there to help out when there's a spot of bother. Pat is accompanied everywhere by his black-and-white cat Jess as he delivers the letters and parcels to the residents of Greendale. There may be plenty of mail but there's always time to stop for a chat with Mrs Goggins the Postmistress, or to Peter Fogg or the Reverend Timms. Pat's endearing personality has made him extremely popular with children around the world.

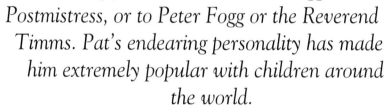

POSTMAN PAT™
© Woodland Animations Ltd 1998
Licensed by Copyrights

Letter Kit

Here's a folder for a child who likes sending or receiving letters. The chart can be found on page 89.

Materials: 20 x 24 cm white Aida fabric with 11 thread groups per inch; sturdy white card; coloured card; double-sided tape; bookbinding tape; ribbon; DMC embroidery threads listed.

Stitch count: 78H x 58W

Directions: Stitch the design in the centre of the Aida fabric and press flat. Cut two pieces of sturdy white card, each 23 x 27.5 cm. Lay them beside each other with a 3 mm gap separating the long edges and then tape them together with bookbinding tape to form a spine. Position double-sided tape on one side of the folder and stick down the stitched design so that it is centred.

Cut two 30-cm lengths of ribbon and tape one on the front card and one on the back, in the centre of the unbound long edge.

Cut two pieces of coloured card, each 23 x 27.5 cm in size. Cut a window, 15 x 19.5 cm in one piece of card to frame the cross-stitch. Stick double-sided tape at the edges of the white card and around the window on the back of the frame. Position the frame over the design and stick it down. Cover the back with the second sheet of coloured card.

Cut two pieces of coloured card, each 10 x 20 cm in size. Open the folder and position these as pockets, one on each side, towards the bottom. Apply double-sided tape or glue around the sides and base and stick them down. These form pockets for holding notepaper and envelopes.

	KEY for Pat & letters		
	DMC	Colour	Stitches
=	437	tan	48
\	444	yellow	13
⊥	517	navy blue	44
O	721	brown	32
I	738	fawn	419
+	754	light pink	160
<	800	light blue	140
*	844	charcoal	54
X	995	dark blue	313
▽	3824	pink	19
•		white	115
	310	black	backstitch

POSTMAN PAT™
© Woodland Animations Ltd 1998
Licensed by Copyrights

Satchel

This sturdy bag is ideal for carrying parcels or books. It is pictured on page 94.

Materials: 28 x 20 cm white Aida fabric with 14 thread groups per inch; 28 x 20 cm white lining fabric; 52 x 37 cm coloured fabric; coloured bias binding; coloured cloth tape; buttons; nylon tape fastener; DMC embroidery threads listed.

Stitch count: 80H x 64W

Directions: Stitch the design on the Aida fabric so that the 28 cm edges form the top and bottom.

Round off the bottom two corners of the Aida and cut a matching piece of white fabric as lining. Zigzag the edges of the two layers to prevent fraying and sew coloured bias binding around the sides and base.

Cut a piece of coloured fabric measuring 52 cm x 31 cm to make the body of the bag. Zigzag all edges. Sew a 1 cm hem along one short edge. Align the other short edge with the untrimmed edge of the flap section and sew the Aida and coloured fabric together with right sides facing. Press the seam and handsew the edge of the white lining fabric down to cover it.

Cut two strips of coloured fabric, each 26 x 6 cm, to form the sides of the bag. Zigzag all edges and sew a 1 cm hem at one short edge of each strip. Lay a strip along one edge of the body section so that the hemmed end is aligned with the start of the Aida flap. Sew the side strip onto the body section, with right sides facing. Repeat at the other side.

Cut 75 cm of strong cloth tape for the handle and zigzag the ends to prevent fraying. Pin and sew each end inside the bag sides, allowing a 4 cm overlap for strength.

Cut two 6-cm lengths of cloth tape and zigzag the ends. Fold and sew a 2 cm hem on one end of each, then sew a decorative button on one side and a square of nylon tape fastener (or a snap fastener) on the other. Sew the other end of the tape onto the back of the satchel flap, so that the two tapes are evenly positioned. Sew the other section of nylon tape on the bag, in the appropriate position.

	KEY for Pat & trolley		
	DMC	Colour	Stitches
V	437	tan	219
\	444	yellow	6
⊥	517	navy blue	76
–	606	red	541
▲	704	green	12
O	721	brown	74
I	738	fawn	70
S	754	light pink	246
‰	776	dark pink	4
✱	844	charcoal	355
×	995	dark blue	667
▽	3824	pink	19
•		white	259
	310	black	backstitch

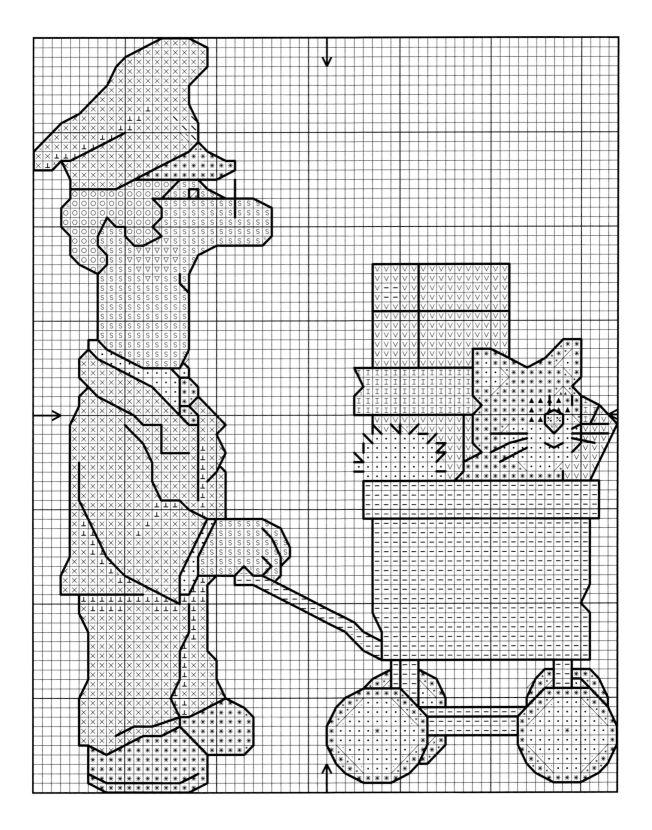

Pat finds an easy way to deliver
pacels on this charming satchel.
The chart and instructions are
on the previous pages.

Here Postman Pat and Jess
feature on a lampshade.
You will find the instructions
overleaf.

Lampshade

Here's a great bedroom accessory, shown on page 95. Measurements are given for a lampshade 15 cm high, but do not cut the fabric until you have checked your frame's shape.

Materials: approximately 52 x 28 cm linen
with 28 threads per inch;
a 15-cm lampshade frame;
interfacing;
DMC embroidery threads listed.

Stitch count: 74H x 55W

Directions: Lay the lampshade frame on its side and roll it across a large piece of paper, marking the top and bottom with a pencil. Allow a 1 cm overlap at one end and then cut out the template shape. Lay this on the cross-stitch fabric and tack a running stitch around it. Stitch the design within the marked area, as indicated below. When stitching, take care not to allow any threads to trail across the back of the work, as these will show up when the lamp is lit.

Cut around the tacked outline, allowing an extra 1 cm at each edge. Fold the hem around top, bottom and one side edge and tack it.

	DMC	Colour	Stitches
		KEY for Pat & Jess	
L	436	tan	24
\	444	yellow	14
⊥	517	navy blue	45
+	721	brown	41
−	738	fawn	251
O	754	light pink	303
%	776	dark pink	8
*	844	charcoal	356
X	995	dark blue	627
U	996	blue	93
▽	3824	peach	32
•		white	292
	310	black	backstitch

Lay the embroidery face down on a large piece of tissue paper and set the iron on medium heat. Lay the interfacing, shiny side down, on the fabric and iron over it for a few minutes (or as per the instructions). The shade should stiffen. Trim away the excess interfacing and tissue paper and remove the tacking threads.

Fit the shade on the frame and glue or slipstitch the overlapping edges so that the hemmed edge is on the outside.

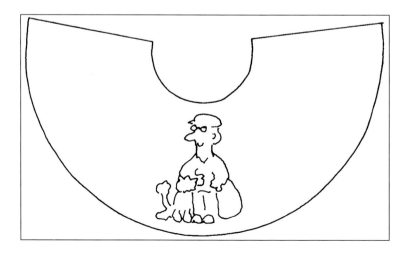

Angelina

Those who don't yet know Angelina have a great treat in store. This is a white mouse whose passion is to dance: in the kitchen, in the school playground, and sometimes even on the stage. She also has all the usual adventures of a growing mouse—being teased by friends, putting up with younger family members—which make her stories all the more interesting for children. Angelina's many tales are told by Katharine Holabird and beautifully illustrated by the deft pen of Helen Craig. The dancing mouse appeared in my first book of cross-stitch designs, and she was so popular that an encore was called for. Once again, the would-be ballerina stars with her small cousin Henry, and this time she has brought along her best friend Alice to perform a pas de deux.

Angelina™ Illustrations © Helen Craig 1983

Tooth Pillow

Here's a lovely gift for that age when the tooth fairy has to make frequent visits; see page 98.

Materials: 18 x 23 cm white linen with 28 threads per inch;
18 x 18 cm backing fabric;
polyester stuffing;
coloured cording & ribbon;
DMC embroidery threads listed.

Stitch count: 36H x 48W

Directions: Cut an 18 x 18 cm square of linen and run a horizontal marker thread dividing the square in half. Stitch the design so that the base lies on the marker thread.

Cut a 7.5 x 5 cm piece of linen for the pocket and curve the two bottom corners. Sew a piece of ribbon to bind the top edge of the pocket. Press a 5 mm hem around the sides and base and then handsew the pocket onto the linen square, below Angelina.

Tack cording (bias piping) around the right side of the linen, with the raw edges matching. Place the backing fabric on top and, stitching through all layers, seam around all sides, leaving a gap for turning. Turn the pillow right side out and fill with stuffing. Handsew the opening closed.

KEY for Angelina as a Fairy			
	DMC	Colour	Stitches
<	307	yellow	29
X	318	light grey	29
−	350	red	35
T	352	peach	111
+	754	light peach	171
O	762	cream	65
N	3747	pale blue	12
•		white	160

Backstitch
350	red	slipper ties, wand, shoulder ruffles
317	grey	other details

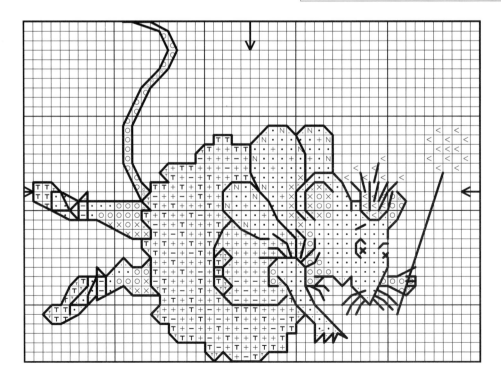

Gift Sack

Henry, Angelina's little cousin, solos here in the costume of an elf. The picture for this project appears on page 102.

Materials: 40 x 13 cm white linen
with 28 threads per inch;
40 x 13 cm white lining fabric;
ribbons;
DMC embroidery threads listed.

Stitch count: 30H x 26W

Directions: Fold the fabric in half to form a 20 x 13 cm rectangle. Stitch the design 3.5 cm from the folded base.

With the design facing inwards, sew the side seams and zigzag all edges to prevent fraying. Turn the bag right side out. Fold over 1 cm at the opening.

Fold the white lining fabric in half and sew side seams. Insert the lining into the gift sack. Turn the raw edge of the lining bag in and slipstitch it neatly onto the folded linen. Fill the sack with small treats and tie it closed with a two ribbons.

	KEY for Henry		
	DMC	Colour	Stitches
O	307	yellow	81
X	666	red	48
U	841	brown	18
+	842	fawn	88
*	906	green	71
−	907	light green	104
▲		white	2
	844	dark grey	backstitch

A curtain tie-back adds a pretty decorative touch to a bedroom. Instructions for stitching it start on page 104.

A gift sack makes a delightful present in itself. The pattern and instructions can be found on page 101.

Tie-back

Angelina and Alice adorn the pretty tie-back on page 103. It's not an easy design to stitch, but it's well worth the patience required.

Materials: 50 x 12.5 cm white linen
with 28 threads per inch;
50 x 12.5 cm white lining fabric;
coloured bias binding;
DMC embroidery threads listed.

Stitch count: 46H x 110W

Directions: Stitch the design so that it is on the left half of the fabric. For a tie back to suit the right-hand side of a window, place the chart in front of a mirror and work the design, in reverse, on the right half of the fabric. Carefully press the work.

Cut a gentle curve at the two bottom corners (fold the linen in half first so that the curves match). Cut a matching piece of lining fabric. Pin the layers together and zig-zag around the edges to prevent fraying. Pin and sew bias binding around the edges.

Cut two 5-cm pieces of bias binding. Pin one on either side edge of the tieback to form loops. Sew in place.

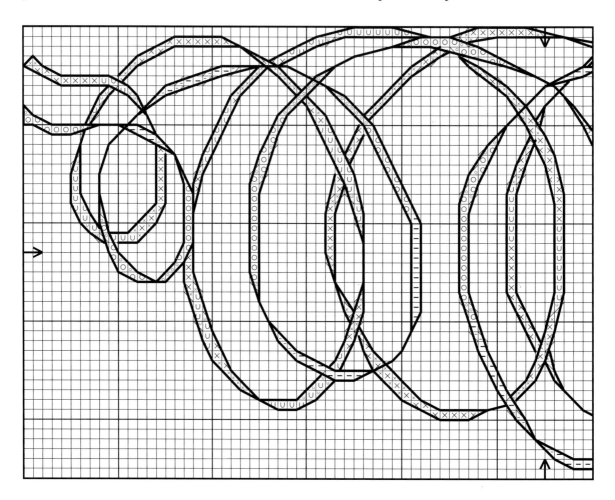

KEY for Angelina & Alice

	DMC	Colour	Stitches
▲	318	light grey	20
O	368	green	242
−	772	pale green	268
Z	841	brown	14
+	842	fawn	117
U	948	cream	245
X	3779	pink	305
•		white	114

Backstitch

988	leaf green	green ribbon
3778	dark pink	pink ribbon
317	charcoal	other details

Angelina™ Illustrations © Helen Craig 1983

Thomas the Tank Engine

This most famous of railway engines was created in the 1940s by the Reverend W. Awdry. His young son Christopher had caught measles and, to entertain him, his father told him tales of unusual steam engines who were given such names as Edward, James and Percy. These tales were to become the Railway Series and when Christopher grew up, he continued the storytelling tradition that his father had begun. The most popular engine among readers was the young and enthusiastic Thomas who runs up and down his branch line with the coaches Annie and Clarabel. There is never a dull moment, what with snow on the line, fish in the engine's water tank, and other technical problems, but the Fat Controller keeps an eye on matters and each story always ends happily.

Based on *The Railway Series* by Rev. W. Awdry
© Reed International Books Limited.

KEY for Thomas

	DMC	Colour	Stitches
✱	310	black	345
−	318	grey	142
O	415	light grey	361
⌐	606	red	50
S	642	fawn	284
Z	702	green	130
T	721	orange	255
<	726	yellow	34
N	739	sand	478
+	813	blue	356

	DMC	Colour	Stitches
U	817	red	117
X	826	dark blue	117
\	827	light blue	37
4	3348	light green	217
•		white	195

Backstitch

DMC	Colour	
606	red	dash lines
726	yellow	dot lines
310	black	solid lines

Pencil Case

Thomas is moving full steam ahead on this classic pencil case, pictured on page 106.

Materials: 25 x 28 cm coloured linen with 28 threads per inch; 25 x 28 cm white lining fabric; 20 cm dress zip; DMC embroidery threads listed.

Stitch count: 54H x 82W

Directions: Fold the linen fabric in half to form a 25 x 14 cm rectangle. Stitch the design 15 mm from the folded base. Take care to backstitch the dashed lines in red and the dotted lines in yellow.

Lay a 20 cm matching zip along one of the raw 25-cm fabric edges, right sides facing, and sew one side of the zip in place using a zipper foot. Fold the fabric in half, right sides facing, and sew the other side of the zip in place. With the zip open, sew a 15 mm seam down each side. Trim the corners and turn the case right side out.

Cut a 25 x 28 cm piece of white fabric for the lining. Fold it in half and sew the short sides to form a pocket. Insert the pocket into the pencil case. Fold the top edge of the lining in under the zip and slipstitch it in place.

Album

This design features Thomas and many of his friends, including the Fat Controller. Here it has been made into an album cover; it would also look attractive as a framed picture.

Materials: 70 x 40 cm cream linen
with 28 threads per inch;
sturdy white card;
thin coloured card;
thin wadding;
50 cm coloured ribbon;
DMC embroidery threads listed.

Stitch count: 110H x 150W

Directions: Cut the linen into two pieces, each 35 x 40 cm and zigzag the edges. With the long edges as the top and bottom, stitch the design in the centre of one of the linen rectangles. Carefully press the finished work.

Cut two pieces of card, each 33 x 27 cm. Mark a line 3.5 cm in from a long edge on one piece and score it with a knife. Cut a piece of thin wadding 29.5 x 27 cm and glue it onto the card, below the scored line. Position the stitched work over the wadding, fold the edges over and secure them with tape at the back. Lace the top and bottom with strong thread and then lace the two sides. Glue a piece of coloured card over the lacing. With a knife, make two cuts along the top spine, each 5 mm, in the same position as the holes created by a two-hole punch. Apply PVA glue around the cuts to prevent the linen from fraying.

Make the back cover in the same way, but using the unstitched piece of linen. Cut pages of coloured card 5 mm smaller than the covers and punch holes along the top.

Cut a 50 cm length of ribbon and thread it through the slots in the back cover, the holes in the pages, and up through the front cover slots. Tie the ribbon in a tight bow to bind the album securely.

If the album will be handled often, you may wish to spray the covers with a protective coating.

KEY for the Engines

	DMC	Colour	Stitches
✱	310	black	1751
–	414	grey	574
O	415	light grey	1041
<	444	yellow	181
H	472	light green	67
⌐	666	red	841
Z	702	dark green	820
▲	704	green	324
+	813	blue	419
U	817	dark red	582
X	826	dark blue	465
＼	827	light blue	28
N	948	cream	13
•		white	142

Backstitch

666	red	dash lines
444	yellow	dot lines
310	black	solid lines

James

Thomas

Perc

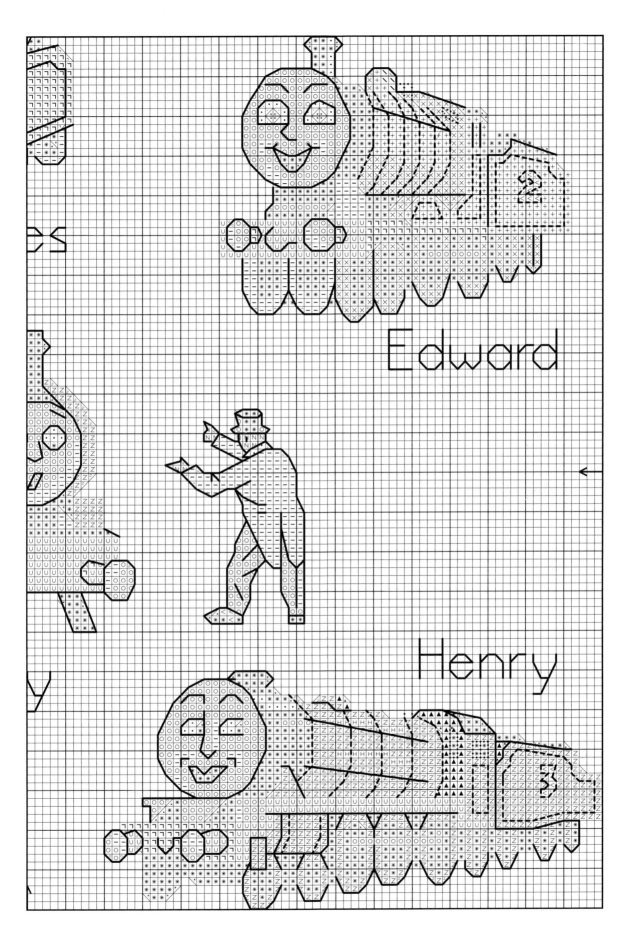

Edward

Henry

Big Bear & Little Bear

The enchanting tales of Big Bear and Little Bear have endeared these two characters to children and adults everywhere. Little Bear is the quintessential child - one who has trouble getting off to sleep, is scared by strange noises, and wants someone to play with. Big Bear is the grown-up most of us would like to be - patient, kind and companionable. They first appeared in Can't You Sleep, Little Bear? *which won several prestigious book prizes for its author Martin Waddell and illustrator Barbara Firth. In this and the books that followed, the lives and concerns of Little Bear and Big Bear unfold gently in the woods and in their bear cave home. Beautifully drawn, the books are full of warmth and reassurance.*

Big Bear and Little Bear
Illustrations © 1988 Barbara Firth

Toy Box

Turn a plain cardboard box into a trove for small toys with a scene of Big Bear and Little Bear heading home after a good day's play. The box can be seen on page 115.

Materials: 25 x 25 cm of white Aida fabric with 16 thread groups per inch; thin wadding; a large round box with lid; acrylic paints; strong backing cardboard; DMC embroidery threads listed.

Stitch count: 80H x 80W

Directions: Stitch the design in the centre of the fabric and press the work carefully. On the top of the box lid, mark a circle slightly larger than the design. Cut along this line with a craft knife to create a hole in the lid which will frame the design. Paint the box base and lid with non-toxic acrylic paint.

Cut a disc of strong white cardboard slightly smaller than the box lid, so that it fits snugly inside. Cut a matching piece of wadding and glue it onto the cardboard disc. Lay the work over the wadding and make sure that it is centred. Fold the edges of the fabric around the disc and use a strong thread to lace the edges together, working around in a circular movement.

Fit the embroidery in the lid-frame. Cut another disc from cardboard and paint one side. Lay glue on the reverse and fit it into the lid so that it conceals the lacing stitches.

	DMC	Colour	Stitches
T	224	pink	43
✳	317	grey	10
U	407	red-brown	14
−	648	silver	240
O	676	gold	1070
+	677	pale gold	360
X	729	dark gold	1207
•	746	cream	63
<	966	green	57
N	3042	purple	44
Z	3766	blue	27
L	3778	coral	40
	317	grey	backstitch

KEY for Big & Little Bears

Big Bear and Little Bear
Illustrations © 1996 Barbara Firth

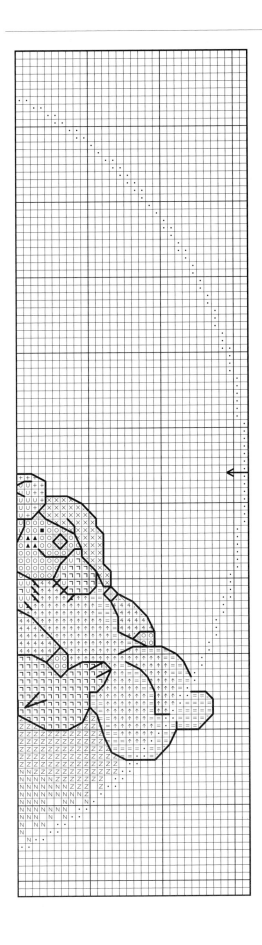

Bedroom Picture

This classic picture of Big Bear helping his little friend get off to sleep can be seen on pages 118-9.

Materials: 42 x 42 cm of blue linen with 26 threads per inch; white board or heavy card stock; DMC embroidery threads listed.

Stitch count: 112H x 112W

Directions: Stitch the design in the centre of the fabric and press the work carefully. Cut strong white board to a suitable size. Lay the work over the board and make sure that it is centred. Fold the edges of the fabric around the board and use a strong thread to lace the edges together—side to side and top to bottom.

Fit the covered board into a ready-made frame or have it professionally framed.

	KEY for Bears at bedtime		
	DMC	Colour	Stitches
■	317	grey	20
▲	407	mushroom	310
S	613	brown	584
U	676	gold	1129
+	677	pale gold	890
⌐	729	dark gold	963
·	746	cream	859
O	754	peach	300
Z	932	blue	197
4	993	green	66
=	3041	purple	100
↑	3042	pale purple	217
X	3328	dark red	180
−	3712	red	98
N	3752	pale blue	511
	413	dark grey	backstitch

Pocket

A pocket can be sewn onto various clothes, such as the top on the opposite page.

Materials: 15 x 15 cm cream Aida
with 16 thread groups per inch;
a piece of clothing;
DMC embroidery threads listed.

Stitch count: 50H x 53W

Directions: Stitch the design onto the Aida fabric, using only one strand of DMC 472 for a pale background. Cut the fabric to the shape required for the pocket, with a 2 cm seam allowance at each edge. Press the seams, folding the fabric over twice at the top edge. Position the pocket on the garment and tack it in place. Secure with stitching around the sides and base, slightly in from the edge of the pocket.

	DMC	Colour	Stitches
■	317	grey	4
·	472	lime	1069
−	503	green	67
+	676	gold	333
O	677	pale gold	229
U	3042	purple	47
X	3773	peach	70
˥	3778	coral	57
	317	grey	backstitch

KEY for Little Bear

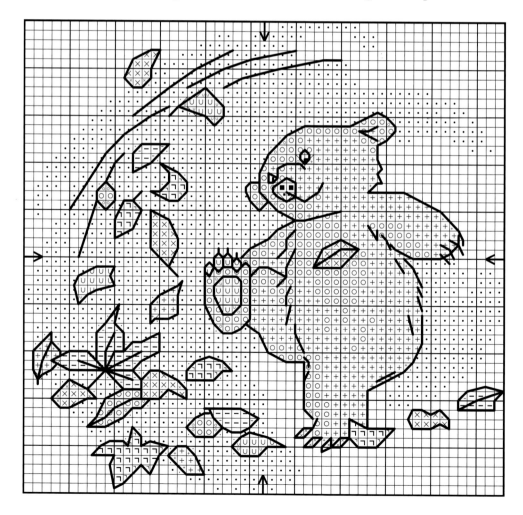

These alphabets and numbers can be used to add a child's name to many projects.

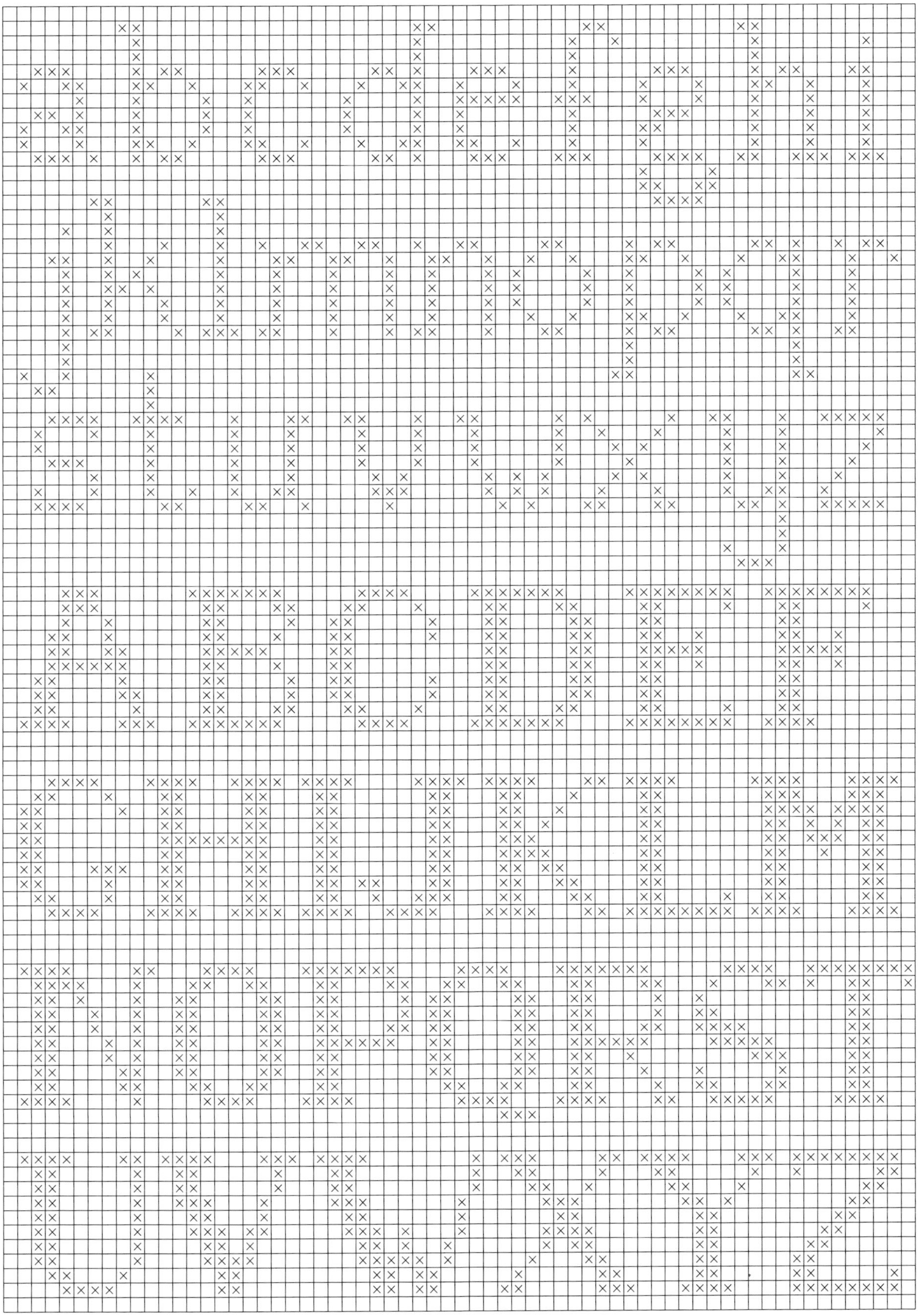

Pattern for the Feeding Bib
(page 33)

Acknowledgements

The charts in this book were created with StitchCraft, a Windows-based software program for designing counted charts. For information on this program, please contact: Crafted Software at PO Box 78, Wentworth Falls NSW 2782 Australia, Telephone: +61 2 4757 3136 Fax: +61 2 4757 3337 E-mail: stitch@pnc.com.au Internet site: http://www.pnc.com.au/~stitch

The Beatrix Potter designs are based on illustrations taken from The Original Peter Rabbit Books™ published by Frederick Warne & Co.
Copyright © Frederick Warne & Co., 1903, 1907, 1909, 1930, 1987.

Ned books are published by ABC, The All Children's Company Limited.

Maisy ™ © 1990, 1992, 1994 by Lucy Cousins. Maisy books are published by Walker Books, London and Sydney, and by Candlewick Press in the U.S. Licensed by Copyrights.

Noddy ™ © Enid Blyton Ltd.

Elmer © 1989 by David McKee. Books first published by Andersen Press, London. Published by Random House, Sydney.

POSTMAN PAT™ © Woodland Animations Ltd 1998. Licensed by Copyrights.

Angelina books are published by ABC, The All Children's Company Limited.

Thomas is from the *Railway Series* by Rev. W. Awdry © Reed International Books Limited, Michelin House, 81 Fulham Road, London SW3 6RB. All publishing rights Reed International Books Limited.
Tank Engine Thomas Again First published in Great Britain 1949 This edition published 1993 © Reed International Books Limited 1949, 1993
Branch Line Engines First published 1961 © Reed International Books Limited 1961
Edward the Blue Engine First published 1954 © Reed International Books Limited 1954
James the Red Engine First published 1948 © Reed International Books Limited 1948
Henry the Green Engine First published 1951 © Reed International Books Limited 1951

Big Bear and Little Bear appear in *Can't You Sleep, Little Bear?*, *Let's Go Home, Little Bear* and *You and Me, Little Bear*, written by Martin Waddell. Illustrations © 1988, 1991 and 1996 by Barbara Firth. Published in the UK and Australia by Walker Books Ltd. and in the USA by Candlewick Press.

Special thanks to Mary Kuitert who stitched many of the designs and to DMC for embroidery threads used throughout.

Index